CHRIST

OUR

HIGH PRIEST

CONTENT

ACKNOWLEDGMENT

We acknowledge our heavenly Father for making us vessels through which the world can touch Him.

INTRODUCTION

To the Son of the living God, Jesus Christ, who got us out of the pit we were in, and through whose Blood we are redeemed, forgiven and victorious over death.

He is the visible image of the invisible God, the visible representation of the invisible, first born of all creation. It was in Him all things were created, in heaven and on earth, things seen and unseen, whether thrones, or dominions, rulers, principalities or powers: all things were created and exist through Him, by Him and for Him.

He was there before anything came into existence and holds it together right up to this moment. And when it comes to the Church, he organizes and hold it together; like a head does a body. He is the beginning, the first born from among the dead, that in all things, He occupies the chief place having preeminence.

"Jesus Christ our great High Priest".

Hebrews 4:14

Seeing then that we have a great high priest, that is passed into the heavens, Jesus the Son of God, let us hold fast [our] profession. (KJV)

In the book of Hebrews, we come across a title of Jesus Christ that very few Christians, denominations, pastors and ministers ever teach or preach about; **"Our High Priest"**. Many Christians know Jesus Christ as the good shepherd, the door, Savior, Lord, King, light of the world, the resurrection and the life, the way, the truth, the life and so on, but not as High Priest.

As believers, if there is a part of Jesus Christ we do not know, we stand to lose the benefits (blessings and encounters), associated with that missing part. For example, if you are supposed to take eight major courses in order to graduate from school, and you refuse to take one, you may end up not graduating. Even if you manage to graduate, you have missed out on something of great value in your life. You will be ignorant in that aspect of life and when the examination of life comes, you may be found wanting. This shall not be our portion in Jesus' Name.

If there is something written in the Bible about Jesus Christ, a title He earned through his eternal sacrifice (death and resurrection) and we do not seek to know and understand what it means and how it affects our lives, in that measure, our Christian lives would be shallow.

Do you know you have a High Priest? A Great High Priest, Jesus Christ the Son of the Living God? In the pages of this book, I absolutely believe that God has an amazing, life-changing revelation, custom-made for you.

The revelation of Christ Jesus as our High Priest, will change and determine your belief system to such an extent that you will have a higher value, respect, honor and exaltation of Jesus Christ. How would you describe your best friend, spouse or child? When we know people well, our portrayal of them is richer and fuller than if we knew them only in passing. So how would you describe Jesus Christ our great High Priest? What impact does your view of Him have on your life?

A servant of God once asked his congregation two questions. First, *"What would have happened if Jesus did not come into the world to die and be raised up from the dead?"* Many answered by saying that man would be forever doomed, there will be total chaos, hopelessness, and man would be eternally condemned.

Secondly he asked, *"Does having Jesus as our High Priest change anything or affect our intimacy with God?"* Many replied by saying that having Him as our High Priest does not really change anything; He is just a High Priest.

The reason that the Church is still into laws, religion and ritualistic worship is because we do not know Jesus as our High Priest and have not understood His assignment in our lives.

Jesus once said to me. *"Daughter, introduce Me to My children as their High priest. Every time they practice their ritualistic worship, they make it look like I never came, I never died and rose again. Do they think I am seated at the right hand of My Father doing nothing?"* Is it possible that our lives are expressing false insinuations about Jesus Christ? We must ask ourselves this question as we grow in our walk with God. Our actions tell more about our Christianity than our intentions.

In order to help us appreciate the full extent of Jesus Christ as our High Priest, this book has been divided into three parts.

The first part reminds us of our human nature, and how man is desperately in need of a Savior. Without this understanding, we would never see the need for a High Priest, talk less of being blessed by His ministry.

The second part opens us up to the concept of priesthood which had always been in play even before the formal ordination of priests by Moses. Did you know that there were other priests even before the advent of a priestly office? This would be revealed to us in this book.

The third and final part opens up the mysteries and realities of Jesus Christ as our High Priest, and how the Church has been missing out on the goodies of His Priesthood.

Jesus Christ longs for us to know Him in totality. As you turn these pages, get ready to meet Him again and again as you begin to see Him in a whole new light. This revelation will change the way you pray, the way you live, the way you see and understand the world around you. Until you know Him as your High Priest you will never become all that He created you to be.

Allow the Holy Spirit help you reach into God, His very nature and complex inner workings of His heart. Let Him create His imprints in your heart, thereby giving you God's best and God's rest. Get ready for an encounter of a lifetime.

PART ONE

UNDERSTANDING THE NATURE OF MAN

CHAPTER ONE
The Beginning

Many ask the question: *"Why did God create the Earth? Why Earth?"*

Isaiah 45:18

For thus saith the LORD that created the heavens; God himself that formed the earth and made it; he hath established it, he created it not in vain, he formed it to be inhabited: I [am] the LORD; and [there is] none else. (KJV)

FOR WHO?

Psalm 115:16

The heaven, [even] the heavens, [are] the LORD'S: but the earth hath he given to the children of men. (KJV)

So, man is the reason for the creation of the earth.

WHY MAN?

Revelation 21:3

And I heard a great voice out of heaven saying, Behold, the tabernacle of God [is] with men, and he will dwell with them, and they shall be his people, and God himself shall be with them, [and be] their God. (KJV)

From the very beginning of the creation, God desired to have a people He could call His own that would willingly love and serve Him with all their heart, soul and strength (Deuteronomy 10:12).

God's heart yearned for children and craved for sons and daughters. Hence, He made man the crown of His creation.

God fixed the planets and balanced the entire solar system. The galaxies were placed by our heavenly Father in their exact locations for His good pleasure (Revelation 4:11). We see consistency in nature because the God of the universe is utterly consistent. Plants and animals were created for man.

Genesis 2:8

And the LORD God planted a garden eastward in Eden; and there he put the man whom he had formed. (KJV)

God planted a garden eastward in Eden (Eden means delight, pleasure, joy and peace), and put the man he formed in it. He loved man so much that God put man in His class, God's class, a personality built with eternity in his heart. A companion and associate of God.

WHAT IS MAN?

Psalm 8:3-9

When I view and consider Your heavens, the work of Your fingers, the moon and the stars, which You have ordained and established, What is man that You are mindful of him, and the son of [earthborn] man that You care for him? Yet You have made him but a little lower than God [or heavenly beings], and You have crowned him with glory and honor. You made him to have dominion over the works of Your hands; You have put all things under his feet: All sheep and oxen, yes, and the beasts of the field, The birds of the air, and the fish of the sea, and whatever passes along the paths of the seas. O Lord, our Lord, how excellent (majestic and glorious) is Your name in all the earth! (KJV)

An angel looked at creation, beheld its wonders and stood in awe of the creator by whose breath creation is sustained. Through the creator's wisdom the heavens were crafted without a foundation. The eternal invincible God that established the earth on waters; solid on liquid. The mighty and mysterious God who sustains the galaxies in patterns. His Name is to be hallowed.

The angel spoke and asked a profound question; *"What is man that you are mindful of him?'* He could not understand what makes such an incredible God mindful of man, so much that He even visits him.

Can We Go Deeper?

Please take note that the question is; *"What* is man?" Not *"Who* is man?" *"What"* is a pronoun used to ask for information about someone or something not understood.

Theologically, we can establish *who* man is but not *what.* What is in man? What deposit is in man that God's mind is full of him? (Note: Man was created naked but not empty).

"Mind" means a person's attention, awareness, will or recognition of something or someone.

"Full" means filled to capacity to the greatest possible extent.

"Mindful" means attentive, aware and cognizant of something or someone to full capacity, to the greatest possible extent. Summarily, could we say that all God is aware of, attentive to and cognizant of is man? I leave you to meditate on that.

Job 7:17-18

What [is] man, that thou shouldest magnify him? and that thou shouldest set thine heart upon him? And [that] thou shouldest visit him every morning, [and] try him every moment? (KJV)

God magnifies man. The Message translation says that God checks up on man every morning, looking in on them to see how they are doing. Isn't that awesome?

Angels come to God for instructions and to run errands, meanwhile man is the object of God's love (Psalm 103:20).

Hebrews 2:6-7

But one in a certain place testified, saying, What is man, that thou art mindful of him? or the son of man, that thou visitest him? Thou madest him a little lower than the angels; thou crownedst him with glory and honour, and didst set him over the works of thy hands: (KJV)

"For thou has made him a little lower Than Angels (Elohim)". The Hebrew word used in the above scripture is not "Angels" but "Elohim", which is plural for God. God the Father, Son and Holy Spirit. The Triune God

In eternity past, before the creation of man, this was the order;

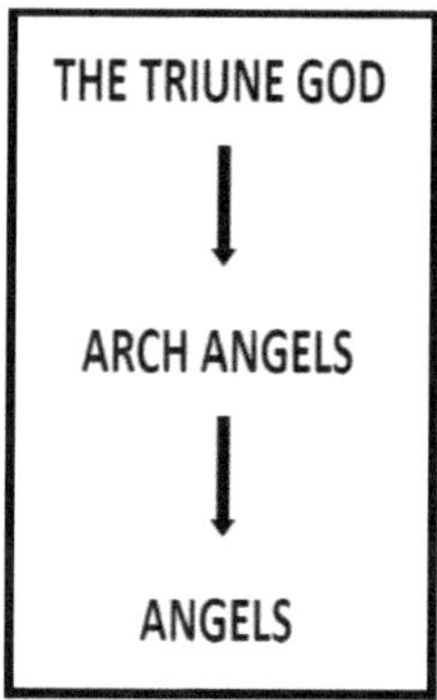

After the creation of man however, this became the new order;

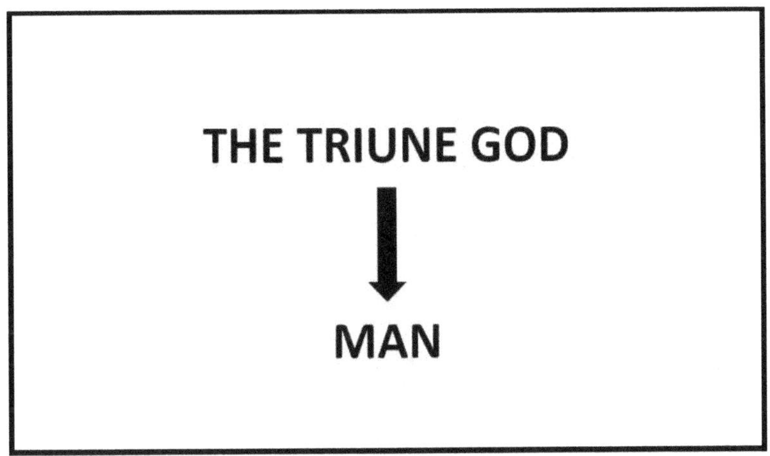

Man was given a position that even the angels did not know existed. No being except God Almighty Himself was greater than Man.

"… and didst set him over the works of thy hands:"

God by Himself crowned man. He did not send the twenty-four elders, nor did He send the archangels or angels to do it. He crowned man. Tell me, who wears a crown? Only a King does.

Revelation 1:6

And hath made us kings and priests unto God and his Father; to him [be] glory and dominion for ever and ever. Amen. (KJV)

By crowning man, God forever fixed the place of man in His heart and plans. What was this crown made of? Gold or diamonds? Neither. The foundation of the walls in heaven are built with precious stones, while the streets are paved with gold. God would never crown the object of His love with something so "cheap".

Revelation 21:21

And the twelve gates [were] twelve pearls; every several gate was of one pearl: and the street of the city [was] pure gold, as it were transparent glass. (KJV)

God crowned man with the most valuable substance on earth, His glory and honor. God's glory sat on man as his crown and clothed him as a covering.

What is Glory? It is the full weight and expression of God.

Psalm 3:3

But thou, O LORD, [art] a shield for me; my glory, and the lifter up of mine head. (KJV)

This was the man God formed in His likeness and image. God made man that He may tabernacle with him. The divinity of God was encapsulated in man. So when Adam spoke, God spoke. That is why he could name all the animals and their names remain unchanged forever.

CHAPTER TWO

The Great Fall

Genesis 2:15-17

And the LORD God took the man, and put him into the garden of Eden to dress it and to keep it. And the LORD God commanded the man, saying, Of every tree of the garden thou mayest freely eat: But of the tree of the knowledge of good and evil, thou shalt not eat of it: for in the day that thou eatest thereof thou shalt surely die. (KJV)

Man did not keep this commandment. Instead, he disobeyed God and fell from glory to shame.

Romans 3:23

For all have sinned, and come short of the glory of God; (KJV)

And when the woman saw that the tree was good, suitable and pleasant for food, and it was delightful to look at and desirable for gaining wisdom, she took of its fruit and ate; and then gave to her husband to eat. Immediately the eyes of both of them were opened and saw themselves naked. So, they strung fig leaves together around their hips to cover themselves.

For me, perhaps the most devastating words in the Bible are found in Genesis 3:8-10.

Genesis 3:8-10

And they heard the voice of the LORD God walking in the garden in the cool of the day: and Adam and his wife hid themselves from the presence of the LORD God amongst the trees of the garden. And the LORD God called unto Adam, and said unto him, Where [art] thou? And he said, I heard thy voice in the garden, and I was afraid, because I [was] naked; and I hid myself. (KJV)

What kind of nakedness would make a person "afraid"? I thought nakedness could only make one ashamed. Adam became afraid because he had lost his covering; the covering of God's glory. From then on, man became a victim of fear.

Genesis 3:11

And he said, Who told thee that thou [wast] naked? Hast thou eaten of the tree, whereof I commanded thee that thou shouldest not eat? (KJV)

Treason and betrayal entered into the world as man spited his maker in disobedience.

What is Treason? It is a crime of betrayal.

A crime is an act that is illegal and punishable by law. It is an act that is disgraceful and immoral.

Betrayal is a treacherous act towards your country, family or friend by helping the enemy. It is also known as disloyalty.

An enemy is a person who is actively opposed or hostile to someone or something. It is anything or anyone that harms or weakens someone or something.

Drawing from the above definitions we can say that man put into the hand of God's enemy, the legal authority and dominion over the universe.

Luke 4:6

And the devil said to Him, "All this authority I will give You, and their glory; for this has been delivered to me, and I give it to whomever I wish. (NKJV)

WHAT CHANGED?

Everything changed, everything!

Ignorance of the gravity of our sin is what keeps us proud and feeling entitled. That simple act of eating of the forbidden tree was so grievous that it compelled God to come to the earth as the Son of man. The fall was so great that it induced the agony and suffering of Calvary (Genesis 3:14-19).

Man was expelled from the Garden of Eden and sent to cultivate the ground from where he was taken. He became alienated from his creator.

"Alienation" means separation from a person, object or position of former attachment resulting in a feeling of powerlessness, hopelessness, and helplessness. Man became separated from God, thereby losing fellowship and right standing with Him.

Mankind, the animal and plant kingdoms, received a new nature. I might be wrong, but personally, I don't think that mosquitoes were originally created to suck blood. I think what we have now is as a result of the great fall. With the fall came curses, pain, sicknesses, diseases and total chaos.

So bitter was the curse that the fruit brought by Cain from the cursed ground was not fit for a holy sacrifice (Genesis 4:3). Man became a criminal, outlawed by his own sin. He became dust that the serpent could feed on (Genesis 3:14). Any time you behave like the fallen man you become dust for the devil to feed on.

The State Of Man After The Fall

Man became mortal, a captive of the devil. His fallen nature is in enmity with God, giving birth to children with the devil's nature and not God's own. A partaker of satan's nature and spiritual death, man became dust, food for the devil. Adam had the opportunity of becoming God's child but he forfeited it and instead became a child of the devil.

Adam became a slave of his environment, so the sun could now smite him by day and the moon by night. A legal outlaw that had lost his approach to God.

Song of Solomon 1:6a

Do not look upon me, because I am dark, Because the sun has tanned me. (NKJV)

THE WAY OUT

Thanks be unto Jesus Christ the hope and restorer of man's lost glory (Colossians 1:27).

Job 9:2-10

"Yes, I know all this is true in principle. But how can a person be declared innocent in God's sight? If someone wanted to take God to court, would it be possible to answer him even once in a thousand times? For God is so wise and so mighty. Who has ever challenged him successfully? "Without warning, he moves the mountains, overturning them in his anger. He shakes the earth from its place, and its foundations tremble. If he commands it, the sun won't rise and the stars won't shine. He alone has spread out the heavens and marches on the waves of the sea. He made all the stars-the Bear and Orion, the Pleiades and the constellations of the southern *sky. He does great things too marvelous to understand. He performs countless miracles. (NLT)*

Job 9:14

"So who am I, that I should try to answer God or even reason with him? (NLT)

Job 9:32-35

"God is not a mortal like me, so I cannot argue with him or take him to trial. If only there were a mediator between us, someone who could bring us together. The mediator could make God stop beating me, and I would no longer live in terror of his punishment. Then I could speak to him without fear, but I cannot do that in my own strength. (NLT)

For man to ever stand in his original state again, he needs a mediator, an umpire, a daysman; to arbitrate between him and his God. One that is God and also man: Son of God ----- Son of man.

PART TWO

THE CONCEPT OF PRIESTHOOD

CHAPTER THREE
The Way Of Altars

The void, darkness and emptiness that was found in creation after the fall of man was so potent that many wise men of old tried to formulate a better type of existence. The harder they tried to sell the fallen lifestyle of man by building systems to sustain it, the more the emptiness grew.

Then alas! Man found the possibility of calling upon the Name of the Lord.

Genesis 4:26

And as for Seth, to him also a son was born; and he named him Enosh. Then men began to call on the name of the LORD. (NKJV)

Only a few men were found worthy of contacting God on behalf of humanity. In one way or the other they began the practice of priesthood even before the word *"priest"* was ever mentioned in the Bible.

Who Is A Priest?

Wikipedia defines a priest as;

*"... a religious leader authorized to perform the **sacred rituals of a religion,** especially as a mediatory agent between humans and one or more deities".*

Sacred rituals of religion in the scriptures are found first and foremost in the building of altars to God. Although there was no formal ordination, some patriarchs of old carried out priestly duties when they raised altars to God in a bid to commune with Him.

These ones carried out priestly duties even before Moses ordained the first set of priests. Man never recognized them as priests, but God did. God recognized their priestly duties and had respect for their service unto Him.

What characterizes a priest?

1. He is a religious leader.
2. He performs sacred rituals of religion.
3. He mediates between God and man.

Based on the above, the very first priest in the Bible was Abel.

Abel

The Bible records Abel as being the first to offer an acceptable offering to God. In doing so, he performed a sacred ritual of religion that typifies him as a priest foreshadowing Jesus Christ.

Genesis 4:4

And Abel brought of the firstborn of his flock and of the fat portions. And the Lord had respect and regard for Abel and for his offering, (AMP)

Hebrews 11:4

[Prompted, actuated] by faith Abel brought God a better and more acceptable sacrifice than Cain, because of which it was testified of him that he was righteous [that he was upright and in right standing with God], and God bore witness by accepting and acknowledging his gifts. And though he died, yet [through the incident] he is still speaking. (AMP)

Abel foreshadows the Priesthood of Jesus Christ. He was the first to show us how Jesus' blood would forever speak as an atonement of the sins of man.

Hebrews 12:24

And to Jesus, the Mediator (Go-between, Agent) of a new covenant, and to the sprinkled blood which speaks [of mercy], a better and nobler and more gracious message than the blood of Abel [which cried out for vengeance]. (AMP)

Noah

The second priest who found favor with God was Noah.

Genesis 6:6&8

And the Lord regretted that He had made man on the earth, and He was grieved at heart. But Noah found grace (favor) in the eyes of the Lord. (AMP)

Noah is a picture of Jesus, in whom God was well pleased.

Matthew 3:17

And suddenly a voice came from heaven, saying, "This is My beloved Son, in whom I am well pleased."
(NKJV)

There is no such thing as meaningless detail in the Bible. Every book of the Bible points to Jesus Christ. As you read the Bible henceforth, look beyond the letters of the Old and New Testaments and look out for the person of Jesus. You will find Him in all the sixty-six books.

In Genesis chapter 6, Noah found grace and in chapter 8, he built an altar unto the Lord.

Genesis 8:20-22

Then Noah built an altar to the LORD, and took of every clean animal and of every clean bird, and offered burnt offerings on the altar. And the LORD smelled a soothing aroma. Then the LORD said in His heart, "I will never again curse the ground for man's sake, although the imagination of man's heart is evil from his youth; nor will I again destroy every living thing as I have done. "While the earth remains, Seedtime and harvest, Cold and heat, Winter and summer, And day and night Shall not cease." (NKJV)

Noah discovered the possibility of an interface, a connection between the natural and the supernatural. Thus he built an altar unto the Lord, the first altar that was ever raised unto the Lord in human history. Prior to this time there could have been altars raised unto demons, devils, gods, fallen spirits of the jungle, mountains, forests, rivers and animals as we see in Genesis.

Genesis 6:5-6

GOD saw that human evil was out of control. People thought evil, imagined evil--evil, evil, evil from morning to night. GOD was sorry that he had made the human race in the first place; it broke his heart. (MSG)

The major sin that breaks God's heart is idolatry. It was the very first commandment.

Exodus 20:5

Don't bow down to them and don't serve them because I am GOD your God, and I'm a most jealous God, punishing the children for any sins their parents pass on to them to the third, and yes, even to the fourth generation of those who hate me. (MSG)

How did Noah come about raising an altar unto the Lord? Nobody had ever done this before him, so how was he able to select clean animals and fowls for sacrifice even when the laws of Moses were not yet given?

I believe the answer is "grace". He found grace and thereafter, heavenly mysteries were revealed to him. I pray in the mighty Name of Jesus Christ that grace will always show up for you.

Through grace, Noah caught a revelation of how to please the Lord. The nomenclature and classification of clean and unclean animals was revealed to him. He had the unction of the Holy One and was able to know things never before revealed to man.

1 John 2:20

But ye have an unction from the Holy One, and ye know all things. (KJV)

Let me give an analogy to explain what I believe happened after the fall. Imagine that a 12-seater bus was involved in an accident (God forbid), and two people died. Four were badly wounded and the last six came out without a scratch. The impact of the fall of man was different for each creature just as the impact of the accident was different for each person. Some animals still had the original operational manual which they had before the fall, while others lost it. Just as I mentioned in Chapter two, I don't think mosquitoes were meant to suck human blood, rather the culture of an insect is to draw nectar from flowers. My thoughts are backed up by this scripture;

Psalm 82:5

*They know not, neither will they understand; they walk on in darkness: all the foundations of the earth are **out of course**. (KJV)*

All the foundations of the earth are out of course including mosquitoes which now suck human blood, rather than nectar from flowers. Noah advanced the initiative of raising an altar, he prayed and heaven responded. He was able to secure a feedback from God resulting in God cutting a covenant with him, his family, the earth and all living things.

Genesis 9:11-17

And I will establish my covenant with you; neither shall all flesh be cut off any more by the waters of a flood; neither shall there any more be a flood to destroy the earth. And God said, This [is] the token of the covenant which I make between me and you and every living creature that [is] with you, for perpetual generations: I do set my bow in the cloud, and it shall be for a token of a covenant between me and the earth. And it shall come to pass, when I bring a cloud over the earth, that the bow shall be seen in the cloud: And I will remember my covenant, which [is] between me and you and every living creature of all flesh; and the waters shall no more become a flood to destroy all flesh. And the bow shall be in the cloud; and I will look upon it, that I may remember the everlasting covenant between God and every living creature of all flesh that [is] upon the earth. And God said unto Noah, This [is] the token of the covenant, which I have established between me and all flesh that [is] upon the earth.

(KJV)

Abel gave the first acceptable offering to God; God cut a covenant with Noah; Noah made the discovery of raising altars and Father Abraham continued by maximizing the principle. See the progression below;

1. *Abel gave unto the Lord, an excellent offering (Genesis 4:4);*
2. *Man began to call upon the name of the Lord (Genesis 4:26);*
3. *Noah raised an altar unto the Lord for he found grace in God's sight (Genesis 8:20);*
4. *God cut a covenant Himself and Noah, his family, humanity, the earth and all living things (Genesis 9:11-17);*

5. *Abraham took advantage of the existing principle of raising altars and lived the life of the tents and altars (Hebrews 11:9);*

6. *Everywhere Abraham went he raised an altar unto the Lord. In no time, the entire middle-east was littered with altars; so much that the children of the bond woman could never possess the land of Israel. This is because a long time ago Abraham had already mapped the land for Israel by building altars.*

Abraham

Genesis 12:7

Then the LORD appeared to Abram and said, "To your descendants I will give this land." And there he built an altar to the LORD, who had appeared to him.

(NKJV)

At the time Abraham raised an altar unto the Lord, the Canaanites who were inhabitants of the land, had no idea what he was doing. They did not know he was mapping the land. Even Abraham might have been doing it unwittingly. He was a father of faith after all, all he did was by faith, not by sight or fore-knowledge of the future. The Canaanites were unaware that the true inheritor, owner and heir of the entire expanse of the land had come. When the cup of iniquity of the Canaanites got full, the land ejected them (Psalm 44:1-3).

Abraham continued to raise altars, and passed on the legacy to his son Isaac, who in turn passed same unto Jacob.

Hebrews 11:9

[Prompted] by faith he dwelt as a temporary resident in the land which was designated in the promise [of God, though he was like a stranger] in a strange country, living in tents with Isaac and Jacob, fellow heirs with him of the same promise. (AMP)

The Bible has no record of altars built by any of Jacob's sons. The next altar was built by Moses when God gave them victory over the Amalekites.

Exodus 17:14-16

And the Lord said to Moses, Write this for a memorial in the book and rehearse it in the ears of Joshua, that I will utterly blot out the remembrance of Amalek from under the heavens. And Moses built an altar and called the name of it, The Lord is my Banner; And he said, Because [theirs] is a hand against the throne of the Lord, the Lord will have war with Amalek from generation to generation.
(AMP)

The way of the altars pointed to man's quest for a relationship with God, someone to fill the empty void in man. Surely, God made a way out for mankind by communing with men like Abel, Noah, Abraham, Isaac and Jacob. These men symbolized Jesus and operated as priests in their lifetime, chosen by God even before the advent of priestly ordination by Moses.

CHAPTER FOUR

The Symbolic Christ

There are many covenants in the Bible namely;

1. God's covenant with Noah
2. God's covenant with Abraham
3. God's covenant with Moses; and
4. The covenant of Jesus Christ.

The covenant of Jesus was cut at the last supper, where he revealed several things never spoken by any prophet before Him (Luke 22:7-28). Though His words at the supper table were never spoken of by earlier prophets, they were not in isolation of the Old Testament.

Everything you see in the New Testament was actually mirrored in the Old. The framework of light (revelation) in the New Testament was already built in the Old. If you can see the framework in the Old, you will understand the plans and purposes of God and how it plays out. Be careful never to disregard the Old Testament, as it contains deep treasures yet untapped and keys to grasping the entirety of God's mysteries. That which God began with Abraham in the Old Testament is fully accomplished in Christ Jesus in the New Testament.

The Bible is a gold mine. Only those that are willing to dig and dig without stopping will find its treasures. God will not cast his pearls before swine (Matthew 7:6). A real miner can be laboring on the mine field for five years to no avail. He comes home black and smelling everyday yet nothing and no one can discourage him because his hope is that he will find gold one day.

Some of the greatest miners on earth that left the mining pit into stardom will tell you how they were in the mining pit for maybe ten years. On their day of breakthrough however, they collected the salary of twenty or even forty years in one day. That is how the labor in the Word of God is.

1 Timothy 5:17

*Let the elders that rule well be counted worthy of double honour, especially they who **labour in the word and doctrine.** (KJV)*

For the written Word to become the living Word in your life, you must stay in the Word and find Jesus Christ in every book of the Bible. This is simply a quiet admonition as we go deeper.

In part one of this book, we saw how Adam and Eve were cast out of the garden, separated from God after eating of the forbidden tree (Genesis 3:23). But the separation was not permanent because God the Father sent His only begotten Son, Jesus Christ to overcome sin and death in the world.

In anticipation of the Savior's great and last sacrifice, men like Noah, Abraham, Isaac, Jacob and Moses through faith, taught their families to offer sacrifices to God. Eventually God cut a covenant with Abraham, and his descendants became Israel.

After Moses freed Israel from Egypt, the house of bondage, the growing family of Israel renewed Abraham's covenant with God, promising to be God's people. However, full of fear and unbelief, they quickly turned to idol worship. Though they were out of Egypt but Egypt was still in them. They were not prepared to enter into God's presence.

Exodus 32:1&7

Now when the people saw that Moses delayed coming down from the mountain, the people gathered together to Aaron, and said to him, "Come, make us gods that shall go before us; for as for this Moses, the man who brought us up out of the land of Egypt, we do not know what has become of him."

And the LORD said to Moses, "Go, get down! For your people whom you brought out of the land of Egypt have corrupted themselves. (NKJV)

They were unprepared to have an intimate relationship with God. They preferred to rely on Moses to commune with God on their behalf, to help the people of Israel draw closer to God. God gave them what they wanted. After all, He gave man freewill right?

God revealed His law to Moses with many detailed instructions about building a holy sanctuary or tabernacle where God could dwell among them. In this tabernacle, Israel, through the priest will participate in special sacrifices and rituals. The detailed design of the tabernacle and the symbolism of the rituals performed within, pointed Israel to the coming of the Savior, the Messiah, Jesus Christ (Matthew 1:21).

The Tabernacle Of Moses

Let us take a look at the Tabernacle to better understand its messianic symbolism. The progression through the Tabernacle is symbolic of mankind ascending from the fallen world into the presence of the Lord God. The Tabernacle was divided into three spaces namely;

1. The Outer Court Yard
2. The Holy Place
3. The Holy Of Holies (The Most Holy Place) (Exodus 25-27).

TABERNACLE

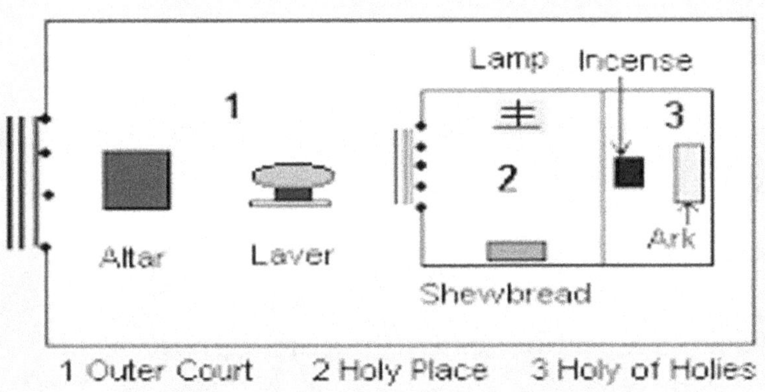

Image downloaded from seek-the-lord.info

The outer court yard invites one to depart from the cares of this world into the space focused on God.

The holy place, lit with the oil lamp (golden candle sticks --- the menorah) can be suggestive of one moving closer to God through the light of the Holy Spirit.

The holy of holies represents returning into the presence of the Lord. A closer look at each space of the Tabernacle reveals more about the symbolic journey towards God.

Only one entrance leads to the outer court yard. Through this beautiful and colorful gate on the eastern wall, Israelites begin their ascent to God. Jesus Christ during his earthly ministry called Himself "the gate".

John 10:9

I am the gate; whoever enters through me will be saved. He will come in and go out, and find pasture.
(NIV)

There is only one gate of entry into the Tabernacle. Jesus is the only way to God.

John 14:6

Jesus answered, "I am the way and the truth and the life. No one comes to the Father except through me.
(NIV)

THE BRAZEN ALTAR

Through the gate, we come to the brazen altar of sacrifice, where sacrifices are offered to God to show devotion gratitude, and to seek forgiveness of transgression, iniquity and sins. Bullocks, rams and goats without blemish were sacrificed on the altar, a shadow of Jesus Christ, the unblemished firstborn Lamb of God; slain for the sin of the world.

THE BRAZEN LAVER

Next we come to the brazen laver, where ritual washings took place. Here the sons of Aaron were washed, anointed and clothed in priestly garments. The priests would wash their hands and feet before performing sacrifices and entering into the holy place. The cleansing water at the brazen laver is a picture of God's Word which is the living water in which we are washed, cleansed and filled.

Ephesians 5:26

to make her holy, cleansing her by the washing with water through the word, (NIV)

THE HOLY PLACE

At the holy place, we move into a symbolic ascension closer to the presence of God. On the right hand is the table of shewbread, where twelve (12) loaves of bread were kept by the priest every Sabbath. The number "twelve" represents the 12 tribes of Israel. The showbread serves as a reminder to be spiritually nourished by the Word which is Jesus who declared that he is the Bread of life (John 6:48).

John 6:51

I am the Bread--living Bread!-who came down out of heaven. Anyone who eats this Bread will live--and forever! The Bread that I present to the world so that it can eat and live is myself, this flesh-and-blood self." (MSG)

On the left side is the golden menorah or golden oil lampstand. The menorah has seven branches each decorated with almond buds, flowers and blossoms. Every evening the priest will trim and refill the lampstand, making sure that the lamps were burning with pure olive oil. This is the only source of light for the holy place and can serve as a reminder of Jesus Christ the light of the world.

John 8:12

Once more Jesus addressed the crowd. He said, I am the Light of the world. He who follows Me will not be walking in the dark, but will have the Light which is Life. (AMP)

Still in the holy place is the altar of incense where the priest burns incense every morning and evening in front of the veil that connects to the holy of holies. The altar's position before the holy of holies shows the importance of prayers in preparing to enter into the Lord's presence. Just as the sweet smoke of incense (frankincense) rises heavenward, so also the prayers of the righteous rise up to God drawing them closer to Him.

THE HOLY OF HOLIES (THE MOST HOLY PLACE)

The colorful veil separates the holy place from the holy of holies. Embroidered on the veil are figures called the Cherubim, who symbolically guard the ark of God's presence. When Jesus was crucified, the veil of the temple was torn in two from top to bottom signifying that through the sacrifice of Jesus Christ, we can go boldly into the holy of holies by a new and living way (Matthew 27:51).

Hebrews 10:19-21

So, friends, we can now--without hesitation--walk right up to God, into "the Holy Place." Jesus has cleared the way by the blood of his sacrifice, acting as our priest before God. The "curtain" into God's presence is his body. (MSG)

The Holy of holies represents the ultimate goal of living in the very presence of God. At the center is the Ark of the Covenant, which is the only object in there, and the most sacred in the Tabernacle. The ark is made from acacia wood overlaid with solid gold. On top of the ark is the covering often called the mercy seat or the seat of atonement with two Cherubim made from solid gold. These Cherubim spread their wings over the ark, symbolically guarding the place where the presence of the Lord dwells. Inside the ark were kept sacred objects namely;

1. Aaron's Rod That Budded
2. The Golden Pot Of Manna
3. And the Stone Tables of the Law given to Moses on Mount Sinai.

Only once a year on the Day of Atonement, does the high priest enter the holy of holies.

Exodus 30:10

Once a year Aaron shall make atonement on its horns. This annual atonement must be made with the blood of the atoning sin offering for the generations to come. It is most holy to the LORD."

(NIV)

Leviticus 16:14

And He Shall Take Of The Blood Of The Bullock, And Sprinkle [It] With His Finger Upon The Mercy Seat Eastward; And Before The Mercy Seat Shall He Sprinkle Of The Blood With His Finger Seven Times.

(KJV)

The high priest sprinkles blood seven times on the mercy seat for atonement. This symbolizes that through the Blood of the Lamb of God Jesus Christ, man can obtain mercy and the opportunity to once again live and abide in God's presence. The Blood sprinkled seven times represents the seven places/times that the Blood of Jesus would be shed, which speaks of the perfect work of the Cross. These seven times/places are as follows;

1. **At Gethsemane.**

Luke 22:44

And being in an agony he prayed more earnestly: and his sweat was as it were great drops of blood falling down to the ground. (KJV)

2. Jesus Was So Beaten That His Face Was Disfigured Beyond Recognition.

Isaiah 52:14

But he didn't begin that way. At first everyone was appalled. He didn't even look human-- a ruined face, disfigured past recognition. (MSG)

3. His Beards Was Pulled Off His Face.

Isaiah 50:6

I followed orders, stood there and took it while they beat me, held steady while they pulled out my beard, Didn't dodge their insults, faced them as they spit in my face.(MSG)

4. The Crown Of Thorns.

John 19:2

And the soldiers, having twisted together a crown of thorns, put it on His head, and threw a purple cloak around Him. (AMP)

5. His Feet Were Nailed To The Cross.

6. His Hands Were Nailed To The Cross.

7. They Pierced His Side.

John 19:34

But one of the soldiers pierced His side with a spear, and immediately blood and water came (flowed) out. (AMP)

These were the seven times His blood was shed. He was pierced for the Church to be born. Remember how God put Adam to sleep and took a rib out of his side so that Adam's bride, Eve could come into existence. So also the Son of man, Jesus, the last Adam was put to sleep (He died) and His side was opened for his bride the Church to come forth.

The Blood and water that gushed out of Jesus' side is symbolic of the birth of the Church. When a woman is about to birth a child, two things give signal that the baby is close; blood and water. Hallelujah, Jesus' crucifixion gave birth to the Church. Praise the Lord, now we see that everything about the Tabernacle in the Old Testament, points to Jesus! He is Lord indeed.

During Israel's time in the wilderness, the Tabernacle moved from place to place as a portable structure. Eventually it was replaced by a more permanent structure called the "Temple of Solomon", built after the pattern of the Tabernacle of Moses. Solomon's temple was the crowning jewel of Jerusalem for almost 400 years, until it was destroyed by the Babylonians.

Several years later, the temple was rebuilt after the same pattern which "Herod the Great" remodeled during the first century. This is where Jesus Christ was brought to as an infant to fulfil the Law of Moses, and to complete God's plan of opening a way back into God's presence through a new covenant.

At the last supper, Jesus taught His disciples about the new covenant made possible by His suffering and death. The following day, Jesus hung on the cross as the Passover Lamb, a sacrifice bringing deliverance to all and replacing the need for animal sacrifices. From that point on, a new kind of sacrifice is now required from followers of God; that of a contrite spirit and a willing heart.

Isaiah 66:2

For all those [things] hath mine hand made, and all those [things] have been, saith the LORD: but to this [man] will I look, [even] to [him that is] poor and of a contrite spirit, and trembleth at my word. (KJV)

In closing this chapter, one important point to note is that the Tabernacle of Moses, is a picture of the cross of our Savior Jesus. The Tabernacle depicted the life of Jesus, and even His death on the cross as in the figure below;

The Tabernacle of Moses

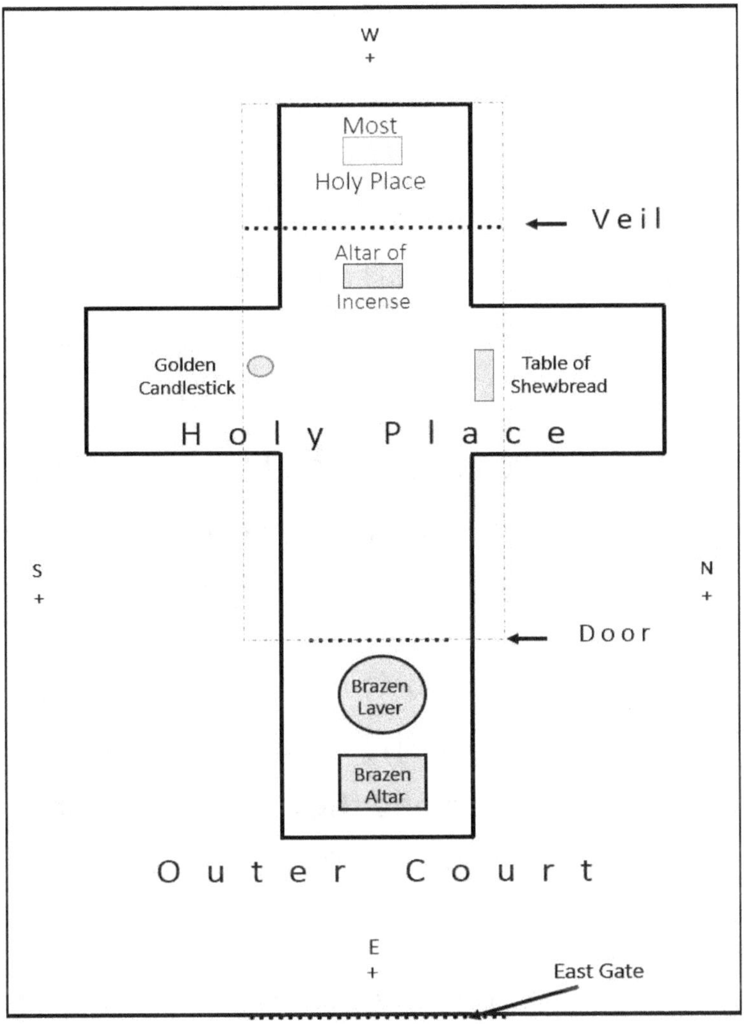

The Tabernacle depicting the Cross of Jesus

The Word of God is indeed, Jesus Christ personified.

CHAPTER FIVE

The Priests

Numbers 8:14-15

Thus you shall separate the Levites from among the children of Israel, and the Levites shall be Mine. After that the Levites shall go in to service the tabernacle of meeting. So you shall cleanse them and offer them like a wave offering. (KJV)

The Levites were separated from among the children of Israel unto the Lord, to serve as priests in the Tabernacle. Among the Levites, the family of Aaron was chosen for the office of high priest.

Exodus 28:1-2

And take thou unto thee Aaron thy brother, and his sons with him, from among the children of Israel, that he may minister unto me in the priest's office, [even] Aaron, Nadab and Abihu, Eleazar and Ithamar, Aaron's sons. And thou shalt make holy garments for Aaron thy brother for glory and for beauty. (KJV)

The High Priest's Office

Hebrews 5:1-5

Every high priest selected to represent men and women before God and offer sacrifices for their sins should be able to deal gently with their failings, since he knows what it's like from his own experience. But that also means that he has to offer sacrifices for his own sins as well as the people's. (MSG)

The priest is chosen by God from among men, to represent other human beings in their dealings with God. He presents their gifts to God and offers their sacrifices for sins unto God. He is able to exercise and deal gently towards the ignorant, the wayward and those that have gone astray, since he himself is subject to the same weaknesses.

Hebrews 5:4-5

No one elects himself to this honored position. He's called to it by God, as Aaron was. Neither did Christ presume to set himself up as high priest, but was set apart by the One who said to him, "You're my Son; today I celebrate you!" (MSG)

No man can take this honor of priesthood upon himself. A priest is a called-out one by God Almighty.

The Priestly Garments

Under the Levitical Priesthood, every priest had a garment which he wore to serve in his office. However, our emphasis will be on that of the high priest. Each piece of the high priest's clothing points to Jesus Christ our Messiah. The high priest wore eight holy garments, four out of which were worn by the regular priests (Exodus 28).

Regular priests wore the following as their clothing;

1. Linen Undergarments.
2. Tunic (a robe).
3. Sash.
4. Turban, all made from white linen.

Regular Priest Garment

High Priest Garment

The high priests wore the following;

1. Linen Undergarments.
2. Tunic (a robe).
3. Sash.
4. Turban all made from white linen.

5. Blue robe.

6. Ephod.

7. Breastplate.

8. The golden crown.

The linen undergarments (breeches or pants) were made to cover the nakedness of the priest from the waist to the knees. The tunic or robe also made from white linen, covered most parts of the body.

The white sash was used as a type of belt to put around the robe, and the turban which was a long stripe of white linen wrapped around the head of the regular priests. The remaining four garments were called the *golden garments* worn only by the high priest.

First of the golden garments was the blue robe which was a sleeved and seamless robe. On the bottom of the blue robe were altering golden bells and pomegranate-shaped tassels made of blue, purple and scarlet wool. The ephod was a richly embroidered vest or apron with two engraved gemstones on which were engraved the names of the tribes of Israel. Six tribes on each gemstone.

Next is the breastplate which had 12 different stones engraved in gold. Fastened to the breastplate were the names of the twelve tribes of Israel. The breastplate was folded in half to create a pocket where the Urim and Thummim were stored. The fabric for the breastplate and ephod were woven from blue, purple and scarlet, wool and white linen.

The last of the golden garments of the high priest was the golden crown over the front of the turban, and attached to the forehead by two ribbons. The crown being inscribed with the words; **"Holiness Unto The Lord"**.

Every piece of clothing including their materials and colors pointed to Jesus Christ our Messiah.

The first four white linen vestments represent purity. In the Bible, white connotes purity.

Isaiah 1:18

"Come now, let us reason together," says the LORD. "Though your sins are like scarlet, they shall be as __white as snow__; though they are red as crimson, they shall be like wool. (NIV)

The Hebrew word used for linen means separation, pure and set apart from the world. All these portray the life of Jesus, who likewise wore a seamless robe all through his earthly ministry.

John 19:23

When they crucified him, the Roman soldiers took his clothes and divided them up four ways, to each soldier a fourth. But his robe was seamless, a single piece of weaving, (MSG)

The alternating golden bells and pomegranate tassels attached to the blue robe, would ring, reminding everybody they were in the presence of the high priest. He was the representative of the

God of Israel. Pomegranate in the scriptures represent fruitfulness, posterity and prosperity.

Deuteronomy 8:7-8

For the Lord your God is bringing you into a good land … A land of wheat and barley, and vines and fig trees and pomegranates, a land of olive trees and honey; (AMP)

There are hundreds of seeds in a single pomegranate fruit, pointing to the atonement of Jesus, through whom we all are made children of God and heirs of His kingdom.

The golden crown with the inscription **"Holiness Unto The Lord"** on the forehead of the high priest served as a reminder that our thoughts should always be holy.

Perhaps the most significant and expensive part of the high priest clothing was the breastplate and ephod. According to the Bible, the stones on the two shoulders were engraved with the names of the 12 tribes of Israel.

Exodus 28:12

And you shall put the two stones upon the [two] shoulder straps of the ephod [of the high priest] as memorial stones for Israel; and Aaron shall bear their names upon his two shoulders as a memorial before the Lord. (AMP)

Symbolically, the high priest carried Israel upon his shoulders as he appeared before the Lord. The 12 stones on the breastplate showed that he was to carry Israel upon his heart, the same way Jesus, on the cross of Calvary, carried the whole world on His shoulders and upon His heart.

The Colors

The blue robe, the ephod and the breastplate were all made of linen and wool. Their five colors were gold, blue, purple, scarlet and white.

Linen portrays separation from the world, while wool signifies the sheep used for temple sacrifices.

Gold in scriptures represents wealth and power. Blue represents all things heavenly, being the color of the sky. The high priest's outer robe being entirely blue, emphasized the fact that his authority was of a heavenly origin.

Purple represents royalty, power, wealth and majesty. Producing purple dye in ancient times was extremely costly and difficult. This means that only the wealthiest could afford to wear the color purple. It is interesting to note that Jesus was clothed in a purple robe by the Roman soldiers before His death on the cross in their effort to crown Him King of the Jews. They indeed fulfilled the scripture concerning Christ's wealth, dominion and royalty. Hallelujah!

Mark 15:17

*And they dressed Him in [a] **purple [robe]**, and, weaving together a crown of thorns, they placed it on Him. (AMP)*

Scarlet or red represents sin, mortality and death. Just as the five colors were fully interwoven and united into a single piece of cloth, the attributes of Christ typified by each of the colors were combined into one to demonstrate the saving grace of Jesus.

The number "five" represents God's grace in scriptures. Each attribute on its own namely; divine, heavenly, royal, immortal and pure is powerful. However, only when interwoven was the true power of Christ's atonement realized. As spiritual Israelites, we are bound to Christ and made one with him because of his perfect life and atonement.

CHAPTER SIX
The Offerings

God authorized Moses and the children of Israel to make sacrifices and offerings unto Him in thanksgiving and atonement for sins. Amongst these are five major ones we will analyze;

1. The burnt offering
2. Grain offering
3. Peace offering
4. Sin offering and
5. Guilt offering

The burnt, grain and peace offerings were voluntary while the sin and guilt offerings were mandatory.

Burnt Offering

The first of the voluntary offerings was the burnt offering.

Leviticus 1:3-4

"If the offering is a Whole-Burnt-Offering from the herd, present a male without a defect at the entrance to the Tent of Meeting that it may be accepted by GOD. Lay your hand on the head of the Whole-Burnt-Offering so that it may be accepted on your behalf to make atonement for you. (MSG)

A male bullock without blemish was taken from the herd, or a male sheep or goat without blemish was taken from the flock. And if the giver of this offering was poor and could not afford a bullock, a sheep or a goat, then he could offer turtle doves or pigeons.

It was a voluntary offering from a grateful heart for God's faithfulness and for all He had done in the life of the giver. It was also referred to as a fire gift, a sweet and satisfying odor to the Lord. The offering was for total dedication, worship and reverence to God. I believe that this was the type of offering that Noah, Abraham, Isaac and Jacob gave unto the Lord in their days (Genesis 8:20).

Grain or Meat Offering

This was also a voluntary offering of fine flour, oil and frankincense. It was a most holy part of the offering made to the Lord by fire.

Leviticus 2:1-3

"When you present a Grain-Offering to GOD, use fine flour. Pour oil on it, put incense on it, and bring it to Aaron's sons, the priests. One of them will take a handful of the fine flour and oil, with all the incense, and burn it on the Altar for a memorial: a Fire-Gift, a pleasing fragrance to GOD. The rest of the Grain-Offering is for Aaron and his sons--a most holy part of the Fire-Gifts to GOD. (MSG)

All the grain offerings presented were to be made without yeast. Yeast was never to be burnt, and honey was never to be added or burnt. All grain offerings were required to be seasoned with salt as a symbol of preservation. This offering had nothing to do with sin or blood. It was a voluntary expression of recognizing God's faithfulness and provisions.

Leviticus 2:11

"All the Grain-Offerings that you present to GOD must be made without yeast; you must never burn any yeast or honey as a Fire-Gift to GOD. (MSG)

Peace Offering

The peace offering was also voluntary, and God did not dictate what to offer. However, there were certain terms and conditions to be met, for the offering to be acceptable. This was truly a free-will offering never imposed on anyone.

Leviticus 3:1-2

"If your offering is a Peace-Offering and you present an animal from the herd, either male or female, it must be an animal without any defect. Lay your hand on the head of your offering and slaughter it at the entrance of the Tent of Meeting. Aaron's sons, the priests, will throw the blood on all sides of the Altar. (MSG)

The presenter of this offering usually decided what he was going to give unto the Lord. However, God instructed that it must be without blemish. It was a thanksgiving offering to God for protection, payment of vows and deliverance from troubles and calamities. It was a thanksgiving offering for all of God's goodness and mercy.

Sin Offering

This was a mandatory offering.

Leviticus 4:1-4

Now the LORD spoke to Moses, saying, "Speak to the children of Israel, saying: 'If a person sins unintentionally against any of the commandments of the LORD in anything which ought not to be done, and does any of them, if the anointed priest sins, bringing guilt on the people, then let him offer to the LORD for his sin which he has sinned a young bull without blemish as a sin offering. He shall bring the bull to the door of the tabernacle of meeting before the LORD, lay his hand on the bull's head, and kill the bull before the LORD. (NKJV)

The purpose of the sin offering was to receive forgiveness of sin for the high priest, the priests, elders and the congregation of Israel. The sin offering did not cover intentional, deliberate and willful sins. This is important to note.

Throughout the Old Testament, if anyone intentionally sinned against God, there was no forgiveness for that. The sacrificial system only covered unintentional sins. If anyone sinned deliberately, he or she was either banished from the camp or stoned to death. The sin of a spiritual leader like the high priest had great impact on his congregation.

Leaders must be aware and protect the calling of God upon their lives because their behavior directly impacts the lives of those they serve. This is quite a heavy responsibility that should never be handled with levity.

Matthew 18:6

But whoever causes one of these little ones who believe in and acknowledge and cleave to Me to stumble and sin [that is, who entices him or hinders him in right conduct or thought], it would be better (more expedient and profitable or advantageous) for him to have a great millstone fastened around

his neck and to be sunk in the depth of the sea.
(AMP)

Nowadays, we hear cases of spiritual leaders who entice members to sin. There was a case of a male children's Church leader, who engaged in homosexual acts with a young boy. This is the state of today's Church. We must not relent on the altar of prayer, as we continue to spoil the works of darkness, thereby taking over the Church of Christ for our heavenly Father.

What Happened When The High Priest Sinned?

Whenever the high priest sinned, he was expected to bring a bullock as a reminder of Aaron's sin of the making of the golden calf (Exodus 32:1-6).
The bullock is the largest and most valuable domesticated animal, a reminder that sin is large and grievous in the sight of the Lord, especially that of a leader. A leader has influence on peoples'

lives, therefore, his sin is more grievous. When he falls, many fall with him.

Paul admonished us to pray for our leaders that we may live peaceable lives (1 Timothy 2:2).

The high priest would lay his hand on the head of the bullock, symbolizing a legal transfer of sin to the animal. In doing this, the animal became a substitute for his sin. The bull was then killed in exchange for the high priest's life. He would take some of the bull's blood to the tabernacle of the congregation, dip his finger in the blood and sprinkle seven times before the veil of the sanctuary, putting some on the horns of the altar of incense (Leviticus 4:1-12).

He would then take the fat of the bullock around the internal organs, plus the two kidneys and burn them on the brazen altar. All that remained of the bullock he would take outside the camp to burn completely with fire. Notice that as he carried the remains of the bullock, he was seen by his family, elders, tribal leaders and the congregation of Israel. Everyone would know that he had sinned and he was also giving a sin offering. His sin was exposed, never hidden.

The effect of sin is grievous, especially for servants of God, who are His voice and hands. When in such sensitive positions, our sin can be devastating. Many servants of God never recover from the shame and disgrace of sins committed. In the Old Covenant, sins were exposed and the disgrace was probably unbearable. Thank God for the dispensation of grace, where we can humbly approach God and He is ever willing to forgive.

Isaiah 1:18

"Come. Sit down. Let's argue this out." This is GOD's Message: "If your sins are blood-red, they'll be snow-white. If they're red like crimson, they'll be like wool.

(MSG)

You may know someone who is in such a position. Instead of criticizing, insulting and taking them outside the camp, pray for them and love them as Christ would. Remember that it was the sin offering that was burnt and not the high priest. If you know a leader that has fallen, take them up in prayers until they are restored back to God. They may not be restored to the same function as before but like a broken bone, we know that if that bone is reset in the proper way and given the chance to heal, that part of the bone will never be broken in that spot again.

It becomes stronger in the place where there was imperfection. Instead of shooting our soldiers, let us find a process of reconciliation where people are not lost totally from the kingdom of God, even though their duties have been suspended or changed. They are still in God's family.

Guilt Offering

Like the sin offering, a guilt offering was mandatory and still for unintentional sin. The key concept that separated the guilt offering from the sin offering is "restitution". That is why guilt offering is sometimes called the restitution or compensation offering.

Leviticus 5:15-16

"When a person commits a violation and sins unintentionally in regard to any of the LORD's holy things, he is to bring to the LORD as a penalty a ram from the flock, one without defect and of the proper value in silver, according to the sanctuary shekel. It is a guilt offering. He must make restitution for what he has failed to do in regard to the holy things, add a fifth of the value to that and give it all to the priest, who will make atonement for him with the ram as a guilt offering, and he will be forgiven. (NIV)

If someone did any of those things that the Lord had forbidden, though he is not aware of it, he was pronounced guilty and was held responsible. If he lied by telling his neighbor that an item entrusted to his safekeeping had been stolen or lost, when found guilty, he was expected to return what he stole or extorted. He was to restore the principal amount and a penalty of 20 percent to the person harmed.

All these offerings and system of worship were shadows of the eternal sacrifice of Jesus Christ the Lamb of God.

Hebrews 8:5-7

They serve in a system of worship that is only a copy, a shadow of the real one in heaven. For when Moses was getting ready to build the Tabernacle, God gave him this warning: "Be sure that you make everything according to the pattern I have shown you here on the mountain." But now Jesus, our High Priest, has been given a ministry that is far superior to the old priesthood, for he is the one who mediates for us a far better covenant with God, based on better promises. If the first covenant had been faultless, there would have been no need for a second covenant to replace it. (NLT)

Praise be unto our Heavenly Father for this new and better covenant.

CHAPTER SEVEN
The Aaronic Priesthood

The high priest was the most senior priest in the Tabernacle and Temple. Aaron, Moses brother, was ordained high priest.

Exodus 28:1

"Call for your brother, Aaron, and his sons, Nadab, Abihu, Eleazar, and Ithamar. Set them apart from the rest of the people of Israel so they may minister to me and be my priests. (NLT)

From then on the, office of the high priest passed on from him to his sons. There are different terms used to refer to the high priest in the Bible. Sometimes he is simply called **"the priest"**, other times he is called **"the anointed priest"** or **"the priest who is chief among his brethren".** He is also referred to as **"chief priest".** All these terms indicate that there were other regular priests serving under the high priest.

Priestly Duties

What was the role of Aaron as a high priest? The high priest offered sacrifices on behalf of the people, because the life of Israel depended on it. God dealt with them based on their sacrifices. The biggest sacrifice offered by Aaron was made on the Day of Atonement when he would go into the holy of holies to represent the people before God.

Secondly, whenever Aaron went into the presence of God, he did so with the names of the children of Israel on his shoulders and on his chest

Exodus 28:29-30

And Aaron Shall Bear the Names of The Children of Israel in The Breastplate of Judgment Upon His Heart, When He Goeth in Unto the Holy [Place], For A Memorial Before the LORD Continually. And Thou Shalt Put in The Breastplate Of Judgment The Urim And The Thummim; And They Shall Be Upon Aaron's Heart, When He Goeth In Before The LORD: And Aaron Shall Bear The Judgment Of The Children Of

Aaron went into the presence of God carrying the whole nation with him. When he went in to pray before God as a person, he wasn't the only one praying, the whole nation of Israel was praying. How so? Because their names were written on his heart. This is very important because when we come to the New Testament, we can identify with what Christ does as our High Priest.

The third duty of Aaron as high priest was to release God's blessings on the people. He took the people's request to God and brought back God blessings. He stood between God and the people as a mediator, foreshadowing Jesus Christ.

Leviticus 9:22-23

And Aaron lifted up his hand toward the people, and blessed them, and came down from offering of the sin offering, and the burnt offering, and peace offerings. And Moses and Aaron went into the tabernacle of the congregation, and came out, and blessed the people: and the glory of the LORD appeared unto all the people. (KJV)

Aaron never came empty from the presence of the Lord, he always came back with blessings and he released them upon the people, thereby bringing down God's glory.

Psalm 16:11

Thou wilt shew me the path of life: in thy presence [is] fulness of joy; at thy right hand [there are] pleasures for evermore. (KJV)

Aaron played a very important role in the lives of the people, making sacrifices on their behalf and taking their requests and petitions to God. In blessing them, God gave specific words of blessing;

Numbers 6:22-27

And the LORD spoke to Moses, saying: "Speak to Aaron and his sons, saying, 'This is the way you shall bless the children of Israel. Say to them: "The LORD bless you and keep you; The LORD make His face shine upon you, And be gracious to you; The LORD lift up His countenance upon you, And give you peace."' "So they shall put My name on the children of Israel, and I will bless them." (NKJV)

The role of the high priest was a shadow of what Christ is doing for us beside the Father as out High Priest. Everything the high priest did in the Old Testament told of what Christ would do much later.

Hebrews 10:1

The old plan was only a hint of the good things in the new plan. Since that old "law plan" wasn't complete in itself, it couldn't complete those who followed it. No matter how many sacrifices were offered year after year, they never added up to a complete solution. (MSG)

Seeing the shadow of a person tells you that someone is coming. That is what the Bible means by saying that the Old Testament was a shadow of better things to come. The old law code is a picture of the Person of our great High Priest, Jesus.

CHAPTER EIGHT

Introducing Christ Our High Priest

Matthew 1:18-21

Now the birth of Jesus Christ was on this wise: When as his mother Mary was espoused to Joseph, before they came together, she was found with child of the Holy Ghost. Then Joseph her husband, being a just [man], and not willing to make her a publick example, was minded to put her away privily. But while he thought on these things, behold, the angel of the Lord appeared unto him in a dream, saying, Joseph, thou son of David, fear not to take unto thee Mary thy wife: for that which is conceived in her is of the Holy Ghost. And she shall bring forth a son, and thou shalt call his name JESUS: for he shall save his people from their sins. (KJV)

In the Sprit realm, names are given not merely for the purpose nomenclature or identification, but are signets and symbols of authority. Observe the manner in which the Name of Jesus is used in the following scripture;

Philippians 2:8-11

And being found in fashion as a man, he humbled himself, and became obedient unto death, even the death of the cross. Wherefore God also hath highly exalted him, and given him a name which is above every name: That at the name of Jesus every knee should bow, of [things] in heaven, and [things] in earth, and [things] under the earth; And [that] every tongue should confess that Jesus Christ [is] Lord, to the glory of God the Father. (KJV)

This scripture describes the potency of the Name of Jesus. After His death and ascension to heaven, a coronation ceremony took place. This coronation was very significant because it was going to change the administration of the purposes of God, installing a Mighty Monarch in Zion. Hallelujah!

In the book of Acts 2:8-11, we see Peter trying to explain the significance of the day of Pentecost. He did this by drawing political, historical and religious lines in order to capture the attention of his broad audience. His listeners were largely non-natives of the land, mostly foreigners.

Acts 2:8-11

And how hear we every man in our own tongue, wherein we were born? Parthians, and Medes, and Elamites, and the dwellers in Mesopotamia, and in Judaea, and Cappadocia, in Pontus, and Asia, Phrygia, and Pamphylia, in Egypt, and in the parts of Libya about Cyrene, and strangers of Rome, Jews and proselytes, Cretes and Arabians, we do hear them speak in our tongues the wonderful works of God. (KJV)

When Peter had successfully caught their attention, he drew them into the personality of a Man; a Man that is a member of the God-head.

Acts 2:22

Ye men of Israel, hear these words; Jesus of Nazareth, a man approved of God among you by miracles and wonders and signs, which God did by him in the midst of you, as ye yourselves also know: (KJV)

Christ is in heaven today as a Man. He was not a Man before, but came down to earth and decided to be a Man. Even as He has ascended to heaven, He still remains a Man.

Colossians 2:9

For in Him the whole fullness of Deity (the Godhead) continues to dwell in bodily form [giving complete expression of the divine nature]. (AMP)

It is the story of Jesus that provides the possibility of writing the destiny of humanity in gold by His Blood. Ascending into heaven as a Man is the basis of hope that humanity can also ascend into glory.

When the personality of Jesus approached the shores of heaven, a significant event took place; the event of His CORONATION. Jesus was commissioned into three (3) substantive statuses in the spirit realm.

Firstly, He was commissioned the CHRIST, which makes Him the Governor and Administrator of all the plans and purposes of God. He became saddled with office of the CHRIST, to fulfil purposes of God which were suspended because of the fall of man.

Secondly, He was given the status of LORD, making Him the entire Chieftain and Monarch of God's universe.

Thirdly, He was ordained the GREAT HIGH PRIEST, seated at the right hand of the majestic throne of God, in the place of highest honor in heaven. He is an officiating High Priest, Minister of the sanctuary and true Tabernacle pitched by God, not man. A High Priest with an endless, infinite and immeasurable life. He is perfect in knowledge of all things; past, present, future, spiritual, physical, psychic, and is aware of everything throughout the universe. He is perfect in knowledge and power.

On the strength of this status that Jesus earned, a life which God exclusively reserved for Himself has now been extended to mankind. The implication of Christ's Lordship is written upon the current signature of His Name, JESUS CHRIST. The implication of declaring His Name transcends the earth, hell, heaven and time. For eternity, the Name will open doors in hell and in heaven.

Therefore, the Name of Jesus is beyond nomenclature and identity.

Father Abraham

Genesis 12:2

And I will make of thee a great nation, and I will bless thee, and make thy name great; and thou shalt be a blessing: (KJV)

When God was unveiling the context and components of His covenant with Abraham, He said, *"I will make thy name great"*. If his name was simply for identity and nomenclature, how would we explain the doors of favor that open to any individual that identifies with Abraham's name?

Luke 13:16

So ought not this woman, being a daughter of Abraham, whom Satan has bound--think of it--for eighteen years, be loosed from this bond on the Sabbath?" (NKJV)

A door of favor had to be opened, protocols had to be overlooked based on the name of father Abraham.

"His Name shall be called Jesus, because He shall save His people from their sins."

When two or three are gathered in that Name, an authority is triggered that facilitates the opening and closing of things in heaven, on earth and under the earth. That is why we pray in Jesus' Name.

John 14:13-14

And whatsoever ye shall ask in my name, that will I do, that the Father may be glorified in the Son. If ye shall ask any thing in my name, I will do [it]. (KJV)

Our prayers are answered based on the merits of Jesus. We live in a heavenly reality because of His merits. We get into heaven because He went out and we live because He died. We get to be with God because Jesus was rejected from His presence in the horror and terror of Calvary (Matthew 27:46).

This same Jesus is our great High Priest.

Colossians 1:13-19

Who hath delivered us from the power of darkness, and hath translated [us] into the kingdom of his dear Son: In whom we have redemption through his blood, [even] the forgiveness of sins: Who is the image of the invisible God, the firstborn of every creature: For by him were all things created, that are in heaven, and that are in earth, visible and invisible, whether [they be] thrones, or dominions, or principalities, or powers: all things were created by him, and for him: And he is before all things, and by him all things consist. And he is the head of the body, the Church: who is the beginning, the firstborn from the dead; that in all [things] he might have the preeminence. For it pleased [the Father] that in him should all fulness dwell; (KJV)

Jesus at the Right Hand of the Father

The two phases of Christ's ministry as mentioned earlier consist of; the Substitutionary work and the Manifold work.

Christ's Substitutionary work.

The word "Substitutionary" is derived from "substitution" which means the act, process, or result of replacing one thing with another. This means therefore, that the substitutionary phase of Christ's ministry involved taking the place of humanity in death as a consequence of sin.

Romans 3:23 & 6:23

For all have sinned, and come short of the glory of God; ... For the wages of sin [is] death; ... (KJV)

The Substitutionary work was done from the period on the cross until He rose from the dead. In those three days and three nights, Christ did the following;

1. Settled the sin problem
2. Conquered the adversary
3. Made new birth possible, and
4. Made righteousness available

All these He did for every person who receives Him as Lord and Savior.

However, if Jesus had stopped His work after the great substitutionary ministry, no one could ever be saved. Therefore the second phase of His ministry, which is His Manifold work began when Jesus carried His Blood into the heavenly holy of holies, in order to give mankind eternal redemption.

Christ's manifold Work.

Oxford Dictionary defines "*Manifold*" as
"having many different forms or elements. It also means many, numerous, diverse multiple and so on".

This definition describes the Spirit of Jesus Christ who we also call the Holy Spirit. In His manifold work, He is everywhere. Meanwhile during His Substitutionary work, his omnipresence was limited because the Holy Spirit had not yet been given.

John 7:39

But He was speaking here of the Spirit, Whom those who believed (trusted, had faith) in Him were afterward to receive. For the [Holy] Spirit had not yet been given, because Jesus was not yet glorified (raised to honor). (AMP)

Right now, Christ is inside everyone at the same time. He is in someone, somewhere in England, as equally as He is inside of me here in Nigeria. In John 14:12, Jesus said that we would do greater works than He did on earth. It is His manifold power that enables every believer to do greater works because the things that Jesus did not do in flesh, now He is doing in the Spirit through us.

Every believer is ordained to do greater works than Jesus indeed.

This second phase of Christ's ministry is His current assignment beside the Father as our High Priest.

Ponder on this scripture;

John 20:15-17

*Jesus saith unto her, Woman, why weepest thou? whom seekest thou? She, supposing him to be the gardener, saith unto him, Sir, if thou have borne him hence, tell me where thou hast laid him, and I will take him away. Jesus saith unto her, Mary. She turned herself, and saith unto him, Rabboni; which is to say, Master. Jesus saith unto her, **Touch me not**; for I am not yet ascended to my Father: but go to my brethren, and say unto them, I ascend unto my Father, and your Father; and [to] my God, and your God. (KJV)*

What did Jesus mean by saying, "Touch me not; for I am not yet ascended to my Father?"

He had not carried His Blood into heaven yet, to seal the document of our redemption and meet the claims of justice that were yet to be met. Jesus died as a lamb but He arose as our Lord and great High Priest; Lord with absolute mastery and dominion.

Matthew 28:6

He is not here: for he is risen, as he said. Come, see the place where the Lord lay. (KJV)

Jesus conquered the dark forces of satan, dealt with the sin problem and redeemed humanity, thereby making eternal life a possibility. The claims of Justice have been met, and Jesus is risen as the Lord and High Priest of a new covenant. This new covenant deals with sons, not servants. It is a new law, not of death, but of life.

Romans 8:2

For the law of the Spirit of life in Christ Jesus hath made me free from the law of sin and death. (KJV)

After carrying His Blood into the heaven Jesus took on the assignment of a mediator.

Hebrews 9:12

He went once for all into the [Holy of] Holies [of heaven], not by virtue of the blood of goats and calves [by which to make reconciliation between God and man], but His own blood, having found and secured a complete redemption (an everlasting release for us). (AMP)

By His Blood, He paid the price to set us free once and for all.

Hebrews 9:24-26

For Christ (the Messiah) has not entered into a sanctuary made with [human] hands, only a copy and pattern and type of the true one, but [He has entered] into heaven itself, now to appear in the [very] presence of God on our behalf. Nor did He [enter into the heavenly sanctuary to] offer Himself regularly again and again, as the high priest enters the [Holy of] Holies every year with blood not his

own. For then would He often have had to suffer [over and over again] since the foundation of the world. But as it now is, He has once for all at the consummation and close of the ages appeared to put away and abolish sin by His sacrifice [of Himself].
(AMP)

Right now, the sacrifices of the law code and levitical priesthood have been fulfilled in Christ Jesus. They are no longer operative and Jesus has become our High Priest. Amen!

PART THREE

THE REALITIES OF CHRIST'S PRIESTHOOD

CHAPTER NINE

Reality One: Jesus Christ Our High Priest After the Order of Melchizedek

Jesus Christ our great High Priest is not a Priest *"in"* or *"from"* the order of Melchizedek, but a Priest *"after"* the order of Melchizedek. The word "after" connotes a similitude or type of something.

Four passages in the Bible talk about Melchizedek. The first time he showed up was in Genesis 14:18-19.

Genesis 14:14-20

And when Abram heard that his brother was taken captive, he armed his trained [servants], born in his own house, three hundred and eighteen, and pursued [them] unto Dan. And he divided himself against them, he and his servants, by night, and smote them, and pursued them unto Hobah, which

[is] on the left hand of Damascus. And he brought back all the goods, and also brought again his brother Lot, and his goods, and the women also, and the people. And the king of Sodom went out to meet him after his return from the slaughter of Chedorlaomer, and of the kings that [were] with him, at the valley of Shaveh, which [is] the king's dale. **And Melchizedek king of Salem brought forth bread and wine: and he [was] the priest of the most high God. And he blessed him, and said, Blessed [be] Abram of the most high God, possessor of heaven and earth:** And blessed be the most high God, which hath delivered thine enemies into thy hand. And he gave him tithes of all.(KJV)

The second passage in which we find Melchizedek is in Psalm 110:4.

Psalm 110:4

The LORD hath sworn, and will not repent, Thou [art] a priest for ever after the order of Melchizedek.

(KJV)

Psalm 110 is a messianic psalm and is actually the most popular psalm referenced in the New Testament. Jesus quoted Psalm 110 is several scriptures such as Matthew 22:44; Mark 12:36 and Luke 20:42-43. Peter quoted it in Acts 2:34 and Hebrews 1:13 also refers to it.

Thirdly, we see Melchizedek in the book of Hebrews;

Hebrews 5:6&10

As He also says in another place: "You are a priest forever According to the order of Melchizedek"; called by God as High Priest "according to the order of Melchizedek," (NKJV)

Hebrews 6:20

where the forerunner has entered for us, even Jesus, having become High Priest forever according to the order of Melchizedek. (NKJV)

It is in Hebrews chapter 7 that we have a more detailed information about Melchizedek. Please note that our focus is on Jesus, as these scriptures only describe the type of priesthood which Jesus has, quite different from the Aaronic priesthood. Let's go into Hebrews 7;

Hebrews 7:1-10

For this Melchizedek, king of Salem, priest of the Most High God, who met Abraham returning from the slaughter of the kings and blessed him, to whom also Abraham gave a tenth part of all, first being translated "king of righteousness," and then also king of Salem, meaning "king of peace," without father, without mother, without genealogy, having neither beginning of days nor end of life, but made like the Son of God, remains a priest continually. Now consider how great this man was, to whom even the patriarch Abraham gave a tenth of the spoils. And indeed those who are of the sons of Levi, who receive the priesthood, have a commandment to receive tithes from the people according to the law, that is, from their brethren, though they have come from the loins of Abraham; but he whose genealogy is not derived from them received tithes from Abraham and blessed him who had the promises. Now beyond all contradiction the lesser is blessed by the better. Here mortal men receive tithes, but there he receives them, of whom it is witnessed that he lives. Even Levi, who receives tithes, paid tithes through Abraham, so to speak, for he was still in the loins of his father when Melchizedek met him. (NKJV)

The character of Melchizedek is one of the most fascinating ones in the Bible. "*Melchizedek*" is a dual name, translated thus; Melek – King, Zedek – Righteousness. He was the King of Salem. Salem is a geographical location which corresponds to the modern day Hebrew word "shalom", meaning "peace".

We can therefore conclude that Melchizedek was a King; King of Salem and King of Righteousness.

Psalm 76:2

In Salem also is His tabernacle, And His dwelling place in Zion. (NKJV)

Melchizedek was neither Jewish nor Levitical. He was a priest of the Most High God. Melchizedek was a King-Priest.

In the scriptures we have men that were both Priest and Prophet like Samuel. Prophet and King like David. But never King and Priest. Only Melchizedek and Jesus Christ hold both offices of King and Priest at the same time.

You will notice that even under the law of Moses, these two offices were separated. Priesthood went to the tribe of Levi while Kingship went to the tribe of Judah. These two titles were not allowed to interchange.

Two kings that offered sacrifices as priests were punished severely in the Bible. They are King Saul and Uzziah.

1 Samuel 13:8-14

He waited seven days, the time set by Samuel. Samuel failed to show up at Gilgal, and the soldiers were slipping away, right and left. So Saul took charge: "Bring me the burnt offering and the peace offerings!" He went ahead and sacrificed the burnt offering. No sooner had he done it than Samuel showed up! Saul greeted him. Samuel said, "What on earth are you doing?" Saul answered, "When I saw I was losing my army from under me, and that you hadn't come when you said you would, and that the Philistines were poised at Micmash, I said, "The Philistines are about to come down on me in Gilgal, and I haven't yet come before GOD asking for his help.' So I took things into my own hands, and sacrificed the burnt offering." "That was a fool thing to do," Samuel said to Saul. "If you had kept the

*appointment that your GOD commanded, by now
GOD would have set a firm and lasting foundation
under your kingly rule over Israel. As it is, your kingly
rule is already falling to pieces. GOD is out looking
for your replacement right now. This time he'll do
the choosing. When he finds him, he'll appoint him
leader of his people. And all because you didn't keep
your appointment with GOD!" (MSG)*

Though Saul was losing his army, he forgot that they were not the ones that made him king. He disobeyed the commandment of the Lord by offering a burnt and peace offering which is the sole duty of the Levitical priest. Saul lost his life, family and his kingdom because of this.

2 Chronicles 26:18-21

*They confronted Uzziah: "You must not, you cannot
do this, Uzziah--only the Aaronite priests, especially
consecrated for the work, are permitted to burn
incense. Get out of God's Temple; you are unfaithful
and a disgrace!" But Uzziah, censer in hand, was*

already in the middle of doing it and angrily rebuffed the priests. He lost his temper; angry words were exchanged--and then, even as they quarreled, a skin disease appeared on his forehead. As soon as they saw it, the chief priest Azariah and the other priests got him out of there as fast as they could. He hurried out--he knew that GOD then and there had given him the disease. Uzziah had his skin disease for the rest of his life and had to live in quarantine; he was not permitted to set foot in The Temple of GOD. His son Jotham, who managed the royal palace, took over the government of the country. (MSG)

King Uzziah was a leper to the day of his death, lived in a separate house, isolated from the temple of the Lord because he tried to be a priest.

This is a very important principle of life;

Never get out of your God ordained function, whatever it may be, so as not to be struck with leprosy. The leprosy may manifest as spiritual one, not visible to the human eyes.

No one could be a King and a Priest, no one except Melchizedek in the Old Testament and Jesus in the New Testament.

When Melchizedek met with the patriarch Abraham, he gave Abraham bread and wine just as Jesus Christ at the last supper gave His disciples bread and wine.

Matthew 26:26-28

And as they were eating, Jesus took bread, and blessed [it], and brake [it], and gave [it] to the disciples, and said, Take, eat; this is my body. And he took the cup, and gave thanks, and gave [it] to them, saying, Drink ye all of it; For this is my blood of the new testament, which is shed for many for the remission of sins. (KJV)

He gave them His flesh and Blood saying, *"Here is the priesthood of Melchizedek restored in Me"*. Praise our Master Jesus!

After Abraham's encounter with Melchizedek in Genesis 14, his life changed forever. In Genesis 15, the Lord God met with him and cut a covenant with him and his seed forever.

What is a Covenant? It is the most solemn and binding form of commitment that the Bible acknowledges for a lasting relationship. Covenants are usually cut, which suggests a sharp knife and shedding of blood. In cutting this covenant with Abraham, God sealed His relationship with him forever in total commitment (Genesis 5:8-18).

Abraham was instructed by God to do something which was a custom those days in the middle-east. He was asked to offer certain animals as sacrifice because without such sacrifice and shedding of blood, a covenant could not be cut.

Abraham brought a 3-year old heifer, a 3-year old she-goat, a 3-year old ram, a turtle dove and a young pigeon. Five (5) items. He took all these and killed them, cutting each one of the three animals (heifer, she-goat and ram) down in the middle (into halves). He laid each half opposite the other, but the turtle dove and pigeon he did not divide.

The acceptable way to cut a covenant was for the two parties involved to pass in-between the cut halves. Abraham passed in-between the cut halves and Genesis 15:17 tells us how God also passed as a burning lamp between the pieces.

Abraham passing through the sacrifice, symbolizes his acknowledgement of being dead to himself but alive to God, the second party involved in the covenant. So Abraham renounced his life, to live in covenant and total commitment to God.

Similarly, God, in passing through the sacrifice, did the same thing; thereby signifying that each party could lay claim on what the other owned. This covenant was sealed in Genesis 17 by circumcision.

On the basis of this covenant, God asked Abraham to sacrifice his only beloved son Isaac. Abraham obeyed without arguing, begging or praying to God to change His mind. He judged God faithful, reasoning that God was able to raise his son up even from among the dead, the ultimate test of the covenant.

Genesis 22:2; 9-12

And he said, Take now thy son, thine only [son] Isaac, whom thou lovest, and get thee into the land of Moriah; and offer him there for a burnt offering upon one of the mountains which I will tell thee of.

And they came to the place which God had told him of; and Abraham built an altar there, and laid the wood in order, and bound Isaac his son, and laid him on the altar upon the wood. And Abraham stretched forth his hand, and took the knife to slay his son. And the angel of the LORD called unto him out of heaven, and said, Abraham, Abraham: and he said, Here [am] I. And he said, Lay not thine hand upon the lad, neither do thou any thing unto him: for now

I know that thou fearest God, seeing thou hast not withheld thy son, thine only [son] from me. (KJV)

Years later when Abraham and his descendants needed a sacrifice for the forgiveness of sin, a befitting sacrifice, the only begotten Son of God was sacrificed to take away the sin of the world.

Invariably, God was saying, *"Abraham. You were willing to offer your son, now I am offering mine".* Hallelujah!

John 3:16

For God so loved the world, that he gave his only begotten Son, that whosoever believeth in him should not perish, but have everlasting life. (KJV)

Just as grace was a possibility back in the Old Testament: "Noah found grace in the sight of *the Lord*", so also was salvation available. It can be given to anyone that positions themselves to receive. Jesus is not only a Savior, He is salvation personified.

In meeting with Melchizedek, Abraham met with Jesus Christ, the Lamb of God that was slain before the foundation of the world (Revelation 13:8). Because the language of the immortal is in past tense, salvation was a possibility for anybody that could believe God for it even before Jesus came to die for humanity in person.

Ephesians 1:4-5

According as he hath chosen us in him before the foundation of the world, that we should be holy and without blame before him in love: Having predestinated us unto the adoption of children by Jesus Christ to himself, according to the good pleasure of his will, (KJV)

Clueless Devil

God knew us before we took shape, substance and form. He knew us as seeds in the realm of timeless reality. Only a Monarch, an Immortal Being has such knowledge. And this knowledge is not available to our arch enemy, satan.

1 Corinthians 2:8

Which none of the princes of this world knew: for had they known [it], they would not have crucified the Lord of glory. (KJV)

That is why when the devil tries to truncate the plans of God, he is always limited in delivering the final blow. There are several secrets in the chamber of design that was set in motion, of which satan has no inkling. The best he can do is try, but he can never actualize his intentions. The devil is only powerful to the extent which man permits him.

Satan is not a creator, so he cannot manipulate a soul and use the soul to actualize an intention that was not captured in the grand and lofty design of God Almighty. The foundation of the purpose of God reaches far back, beyond the period when time began. That is why only the Immortal King has the original document of events.

Satan cannot terminate in time, what has its root in eternity. This was the message Jesus preached to Saul on the way to Damascus.

Acts 9:5

And he said, Who art thou, Lord? And the Lord said, I am Jesus whom thou persecutest: [it is] hard for thee to kick against the pricks. (KJV)

"It is hard for thee to kick against the pricks". This means it is hard to bring an end to something that has its root in eternity.

In his dealing with God, Abraham found that salvation was available. He is an excellent example of a saved man, a colossus. Thus he became;

1. A friend of God
2. Father of many Nations
3. Father of faith.

He found life, eternal life, when he encountered the giver of life.

John 17:3

And this is eternal life, that they may know You, the only true God, and Jesus Christ whom You have sent. (NKJV)

Abraham was ahead of his generation. He found Jesus Christ, the great High Priest after the order of Melchizedek that changed his life forever. Jesus declared in;

John 8:56

Your father Abraham rejoiced to see My day, and he saw it and was glad." (NKJV)

May you also encounter Jesus as you read in Jesus' Mighty Name.

CHAPTER TEN

Reality Two: Jesus Christ the High Priest with a New and Better Covenant

Let us open up this chapter by reading the following scriptures;

Jeremiah 31:31-34

Behold, the days come, saith the LORD, that I will make a new covenant with the house of Israel, and with the house of Judah: Not according to the covenant that I made with their fathers in the day [that] I took them by the hand to bring them out of the land of Egypt; which my covenant they brake, although I was an husband unto them, saith the LORD: But this [shall be] the covenant that I will make with the house of Israel; After those days, saith the LORD, I will put my law in their inward parts, and write it in their hearts; and will be their God, and they shall be my people. And they shall teach no more every man his neighbour, and every man his brother, saying, Know the LORD: for they shall all know me, from the least of them unto the greatest of them, saith the LORD: for I will forgive their iniquity, and I will remember their sin no more. (KJV)

Ezekiel 11:19-20

And I will give them one heart, and I will put a new spirit within you; and I will take the stony heart out of their flesh, and will give them an heart of flesh: That they may walk in my statutes, and keep mine ordinances, and do them: and they shall be my people, and I will be their God. (KJV)

Jeremiah 24:7

And I will give them an heart to know me, that I [am] the LORD: and they shall be my people, and I will be their God: for they shall return unto me with their whole heart. (KJV)

Romans 11:27

For this [is] my covenant unto them, when I shall take away their sins. (KJV)

The book of Hebrews places a heavy emphasis on Jesus Christ as our great High Priest in the heavenly sanctuary. In fact, the clearest exposition of the new covenant in the New Testament is found in the book of Hebrews. This is no coincidence as Christ's heavenly ministry is clearly and closely tied to the promise of a new and better covenant.

The Ten Commandments given to Moses on Mount Sinai, were written on tablets of stone. However, in the new covenant, the laws will be written on the hearts and minds of mankind. How is this possible?

Hebrews 8:1-2

Now of the things which we have spoken [this is] the sum: We have such an high priest, who is set on the right hand of the throne of the Majesty in the heavens; A minister of the sanctuary, and of the true tabernacle, which the Lord pitched, and not man.

(KJV)

The focal point of this new covenant is Jesus Christ and His ministry of High priesthood. For Jesus Christ to become our High Priest, He had to lay aside His kingly role and immortality. The scepter of the universe was given to God the Father for Christ to take on humanity and be born a man. He became familiar with all our weaknesses, tempted in every way, yet without sin. He understood and knew our frame and therefore offered Himself as our sacrifice, a better sacrifice.

Hebrews 8:6-7

But now hath he obtained a more excellent ministry, by how much also he is the mediator of a better covenant, which was established upon better promises. For if that first [covenant] had been faultless, then should no place have been sought for the second. (KJV)

The old covenant failed, as the children of Israel were content with having the laws written on stones hidden away in the Tabernacle. They liked the idea of God but never wanted a closer walk with Him.

Exodus 20:18-21

And all the people saw the thunderings, and the lightnings, and the noise of the trumpet, and the mountain smoking: and when the people saw [it], **they removed, and stood afar off**. *And they said unto Moses, Speak thou with us, and we will hear: but let not God speak with us, lest we die. And Moses said unto the people, Fear not: for God is come to prove you, and that his fear may be before your faces,* **that ye sin not**. *And the people stood afar off, and Moses drew near unto the thick darkness where God [was]. (KJV)*

They stood afar off, not wanting close relationship with God. Hence His laws could not be written on their hearts.

Psalm 73:13

Verily I have cleansed my heart [in] vain, and washed my hands in innocency. (KJV)

Only God can do the cleansing work on our hearts perfectly in His own way. Central to this new and better covenant is Jesus, writing the laws of God upon our hearts and minds. The law defines what love is; the law is love and God is love.

Exodus 20:1-17

And God spake all these words, saying, I [am] the LORD thy God, which have brought thee out of the land of Egypt, out of the house of bondage. Thou shalt have no other gods before me. Thou shalt not make unto thee any graven image, or any likeness [of any thing] that [is] in heaven above, or that [is] in the earth beneath, or that [is] in the water under the earth: Thou shalt not bow down thyself to them, nor serve them: for I the LORD thy God [am] a jealous God, visiting the iniquity of the fathers upon the children unto the third and fourth [generation] of them that hate me; And shewing mercy unto thousands of them that love me, and keep my commandments. Thou shalt not take the name of the LORD thy God in vain; for the LORD will not hold him guiltless that taketh his name in vain. Remember the sabbath day, to keep it holy. Six days shalt thou labour, and do all thy work: But the seventh day [is] the sabbath of the LORD thy God: [in it] thou shalt not do any work, thou, nor thy son, nor thy daughter, thy manservant, nor thy maidservant, nor thy cattle, nor thy stranger that [is] within thy gates: For [in] six days the LORD made heaven and earth, the sea, and all that in them [is], and rested the seventh day: wherefore the LORD blessed the sabbath day, and hallowed it. Honour thy father and thy mother: that thy days may be long upon the land which the LORD thy God giveth thee. Thou shalt not kill. Thou shalt not commit adultery. Thou shalt not steal. Thou shalt not bear false witness against thy neighbour. Thou shalt not covet thy neighbour's house, thou shalt not covet thy neighbour's wife, nor his manservant, nor his maidservant, nor his ox, nor his ass, nor any thing that [is] thy neighbour's. (KJV)

These laws define what love is. If we love God with all of our hearts and minds, we would keep the first four commandments. And if we love our neighbors (humanity) as ourselves, we would keep the last six.

So, the Ten Commandments define the kind of love relationship which God wants with us, and which He wants us to have with our fellow humans.

Mark 12:28-34

And one of the scribes came, and having heard them reasoning together, and perceiving that he had answered them well, asked him, Which is the first commandment of all? And Jesus answered him, The first of all the commandments [is], Hear, O Israel; The Lord our God is one Lord: And thou shalt love the Lord thy God with all thy heart, and with all thy soul, and with all thy mind, and with all thy strength: this [is] the first commandment. And the second [is] like, [namely] this, Thou shalt love thy neighbour as thyself. There is none other commandment greater than these. And the scribe said unto him, Well, Master, thou hast said the truth: for there is one God; and there is none other but he: And to love him with all the heart, and with all the understanding, and with all the soul, and with all the strength, and to love [his] neighbour as himself, is more than all whole burnt offerings and sacrifices. And when Jesus saw that he answered discreetly, he said unto him, Thou art not far from the kingdom of God. And no man after that durst ask him [any question]. (KJV)

Jesus Christ is the fulfillment of the law.

Matthew 5:17

"Do not think that I came to destroy the Law or the Prophets. I did not come to destroy but to fulfill.
(NKJV)

Jesus enjoined His audience not to misunderstand His reason for coming. He continued by saying that God's law is more real and lasting than the heavens and earth. God's law will be alive and working until its very purpose is achieved.

If you break the smallest commandment and teach others to do same, you will be the least in heaven's kingdom. However, anyone who obeys God's laws and teaches them will be great in the kingdom of heaven.

The time appointed came when Jesus Christ, the Messiah, arrived as our High Priest of better and superior things of this new covenant. Christ went to that great and perfect sanctuary in heaven, not made by human hands and not part of this created world.

He bypassed the sacrifices consisting of the blood of goats and calves. Jesus entered once and for all into the holy place with His own Blood, securing an eternal redemption, a complete and everlasting release for us.

The blood of goats and calves, the ashes of a heifer sprinkled on the unclean, was sufficient for purification of the body.

How much more surely shall the blood of Christ, who by His eternal Spirit offered Himself, an unblemished sacrifice to God, purify our heart from deeds that lead to death, so that we can worship the living God with all of our hearts and minds?

Christ is therefore the negotiator and mediator of an entirely new agreement, testament and covenant. We now have an everlasting inheritance since a death has occurred, of Jesus Christ that redeems, recues and delivers us from the transgressions committed.

Through the Holy Spirit, Jesus cleanses us from sin.

The Purpose of the Church

What then is the purpose of the Church? It is to preach the gospel, telling the world that the sin problem has been taken care of by Jesus Christ our great High Priest. Telling them what Jesus did, is still doing, and is yet to do on our behalf. This new covenant produces holiness of heart and a transformed character.

Old Covenant	New Covenant
Levitical Priesthood	Melchizedek Priesthood
Animal sacrifice	Sacrifice of Jesus. He is both the sacrifice and the High Priest
Earthly sanctuary	Heavenly sanctuary
Man's promises	God's promises
Literal Israel	Spiritual Israel

Practical Application of the New Covenant

How can we enter into this new and better covenant experience? It is not a once-in-a-lifetime experience, but a daily one. That is why Apostle Paul said, *"I die daily"*, the surrender of selfish desires day by day and moment by moment (1 Corinthians 15:31).

How can we become the parchments that Jesus can inscribe His laws upon?

1. **Ask God for help by His Spirit –**

John 3:27

John answered and said, A man can receive nothing, except it be given him from heaven. (KJV)

2. **Surrender your will –**

Philippians 2:13-14

For it is God which worketh in you both to will and to do of [his] good pleasure. Do all things without murmurings and disputings: (KJV)

You surrender your will daily before God by saying, "not my will but Your will be done in my life, family, ministry, career, business and everything that concerns me". No one will be able to speak a word of blame against you. Your life will be blameless, guileless, innocent and uncontaminated, as sons and daughters faultless in a crooked and wicked, spiritually perverted world. Your light will shine forth clearly in a world so full of darkness.

As you wake up in the morning, talk to Jesus Christ, your great High Priest. Give Him your will because He is the only one that can truly help you. Receive grace to yield in Jesus' Name, Amen.

3. **Surrender your mind –**

Philippians 2:5-7

Let this mind be in you, which was also in Christ Jesus: Who, being in the form of God, thought it not robbery to be equal with God: But made himself of no reputation, and took upon him the form of a servant, and was made in the likeness of men: (KJV)

Surrender your mind totally to Jesus Christ. Do this by saying this prayer daily; "Father in the Name of Jesus, please let Your mind be in me today". Stay humble daily, living a selfless and obedient life always.

Proverbs 23:26

My son, give me thine heart, and let thine eyes observe my ways. (KJV)

Give the Lord your full attention and do as He says. The grace to do this is yours in Jesus' mighty Name. Say this prayer, "Father please take my full attention in Jesus' Mighty Name. Amen".

4. Surrender your body and all your plans daily – Romans 12:1

I beseech you therefore, brethren, by the mercies of God, that ye present your bodies a living sacrifice, holy, acceptable unto God, [which is] your reasonable service. (KJV)

In the morning, afternoon and evening (night and day), surrender; total surrender.

Pray saying, "Dear Lord, here are my plans for today, please work them out according to Your plan for my life. I lay them all at Your feet, please direct, instruct and lead me today, in Jesus' Name. Amen."

5. **Consecrate your heart to the Lord daily –**

Saints of God, consecration is a very simple thing when brought practically into our individual lives daily. We shall know far more by consecration than by trusting our own experiences. Every day and every hour, let your heart go after God.

Say this prayer, "Here I am oh Lord, I am Your property. Please take me and use me today for Your good pleasure. I lay my life down at Your feet,

I will have no way of my own in any matter, for my time is Yours in Jesus' Name. Amen"

Let your heart constantly go forth to God for strength and grace every morning. He said in His Word;

Matthew 11:28-30

Come unto me, all [ye] that labour and are heavy laden, and I will give you rest. Take my yoke upon you, and learn of me; for I am meek and lowly in heart: and ye shall find rest unto your souls. For my yoke [is] easy, and my burden is light. (KJV)

6. **Come as you are –**

We can come to Jesus Christ just the way we are. He is the only one that can clean us up, for we cannot clean ourselves up. What the law could not perfect, Christ did. Now He has introduced to us a better hope through which we now come close to God.

If Jesus does not bear your sin and you cannot turn to Him for forgiveness, how then can you deal with sin in your life? In reality, there is life, death and judgment. Christ bore the greatest burden of sin according to John 1:29 and we are free at last and forever from the bondage of sin.

If you have never received Jesus Christ as your Lord and Savior, or if you want to rededicate your life to Him, please say the prayer below;

Lord Jesus, I come to You today just as I am. No more pretense Lord, I need Your help. Please come into my life today as my Savior and Lord. Forgive me all my sins, take control of my life and fill me with Your Holy Spirit. Father please use me for Christ's sake and take full possession of me in Jesus' great Name I pray.

If you just prayed this prayer, I rejoice with you. Welcome to a new found life in Jesus. Please join a Bible believing Church and be planted there. You can also call us on the phone numbers on the copyright page of this book. Congratulations!

7. Never forget the focus, Jesus –

Finally, we must always remember that the focus of this new covenant is Jesus. The reality of His life on earth, His performance, His works, death, burial and resurrection all point to the Cross. Who will write the laws upon the heart and mind of a believer? Jesus Christ will, through the ministry of His precious Holy Spirit.

This is why He told His disciples to tarry in Jerusalem and wait for the promise of the Father. What promise? The promise of the Holy Spirit and power.

Acts 1:8

But ye shall receive power, after that the Holy Ghost is come upon you: and ye shall be witnesses unto me both in Jerusalem, and in all Judaea, and in Samaria, and unto the uttermost part of the earth. (KJV)

What is this power meant for? To do miracles, heal the sick, cleanse lepers or raise the dead? Not entirely. All these miracles and signs existed in the old covenant. The power of the Holy Spirit is primarily to live above sin and bring reconciliation between God and man.

Jesus Christ gives us new hearts and puts new spirits within us. Hallelujah!

CHAPTER ELEVEN

Reality Three: Jesus Christ Our High Priest With an Unchangeable Priesthood

Hebrews 7:23-25

And they truly were many priests, because they were not suffered to continue by reason of death: But this [man], because he continueth ever, hath an unchangeable priesthood. Wherefore he is able also to save them to the uttermost that come unto God by him, seeing he ever liveth to make intercession for them. (KJV)

Jesus Christ is the High Priest perfectly adapted to our needs. We have a holy High Priest, uncompromised by sin, with authority extending as high as God's presence in heaven itself. Hallelujah!

Unlike the other high priests, Jesus does not have to offer sacrifices for His own sins every day before getting around to us and our sins. He did once and for all when He sacrificed Himself on the cross.

The Mosaic Law appointed as high priests, men who were never able to get the job done right because they were limited by human weakness. They were frail, sinful and dying human beings. On the other hand. Jesus' appointment as High Priest is complete and permanent, eternally perfect!

Just as every other Aaronic priest was assigned to offer both gifts and sacrifices, our High Priest must make an offering too. However, His offering was His own Blood. No more yearly repeated sacrifices of goats and calves; no more rituals. Christ has made us free forever.

Hebrews 1:3

Who being the brightness of [his] glory, and the express image of his person, and upholding all things by the word of his power, when he had by himself purged our sins, sat down on the right hand of the Majesty on high; (KJV)

Jesus Christ our High Priest sat down while the levitical priests in the old testament never sat down. They were never allowed to sit down while at work. There were no chairs in the temple or tabernacle. Why? Because their work was never done, passing the baton from one generation of priests to another.

Jesus Christ offered Himself once and for all and He sat down, done and finished. The work is complete, never needing another generation of priests to take over. He is forever the victorious King and Priest.

Christ came with a superior covenant, with the guarantee of His own Blood, a promise made between Father and Son. The Son said, *"I will go, I will die, I will pour out my blood to unleash the power of God in the lives of men"* (Isaiah 6:8). By His sacrifice, the wrath of God has been totally removed. Because Christ has an unchangeable Priesthood, He is able to save to the uttermost, completely, perfectly, finally and for all time and eternity. He is always on the job to speak up for anyone that comes to God through Him, making petition to God, arbitrating and intervening for man.

Because of Jesus Christ out High Priest, we have full freedom and confidence to enter into the Holy of holies without hesitation. Jesus has cleared the way by the Blood of His sacrifice into God's abode.

Come forward brethren, draw near with full assurance of faith, fully trusting in His power, love, mercy and goodness; having our evil conscience sprinkled with His Blood.

In view of all that Jesus Christ has done and is still doing, let us;

1. **Hebrews 10:23-25** - hold fast the profession of [our] faith without wavering; (for he [is] faithful that promised;) (KJV).

2. Give attentive, continuous care, watching over one another.

3. Stimulate and incite love among ourselves through helpful deeds and noble activities, not forsaking or neglecting to assemble together as believers.

4. Admonish, warn and encourage one another in love as we see His coming back is drawing near.

Though we have Jesus as our High Priest, let us not deliberately and willfully sin. If everyone that violated, despised and refused to obey the law of Moses was put to death without mercy, how much worse the punishment for one who tramples underfoot, the Son of God.

Do not treat the Blood of Jesus as common and unholy. Anyone that does this has insulted and enraged the Holy Spirit who is the Spirit of grace and mercy. It is formidable and terrible to incur God's wrath.

Do not throw away this confident trust in the Lord, no matter what happens. Remember that this trust has a great reward which it brings to you. As children of the new covenant, we are not of them that draw back; we will cleave to, trust in and rely on God through Jesus Christ our great High Priest all the days of our lives. Amen.

You have been raised with Christ to a new life, sharing His resurrection from the dead. Therefore act like it by aiming at, seeking and pursuing the rich and eternal treasures which are above; where Jesus is seated at the right hand of God in honor and power.

Setting our minds on Christ, that is where the action is. Seeing things from His perspective, not only from our earthly view. As far as the world is concerned, you have died and your new life, your real life is hidden with Christ in God.

His High Priesthood is better and more permanent with a better sacrifice. He paid with His own Blood and His Blood was higher than the value of man. In other words, He paid and overpaid what was required for us to be saved. He paid it so well that there was nothing left to be paid for yearly, as was the old custom.

CHAPTER TWELVE

Reality Four: Jesus Christ Our High Priest with the Power of an Endless and Indestructible Life, Backed up With an Oath

Hebrews 7:16

Who has been constituted a Priest, not on the basis of a bodily legal requirement [an externally imposed command concerning His physical ancestry], but on the basis of the power of an endless and indestructible Life. (AMP)

If you ask me why I love Jesus, it is because He first loved me and laid down His life for me. if you ask me why I worship Him, it is because He created all things, upholds, knows, accomplishes, rules over, is above and is at the center of all things.

How can these be? It is possible because Jesus has the power of an endless and indestructible life.

I have given my entire life to Him in faith and trust that he is superior to all other claims in the world. He is infinite, eternal over all things and worthy above all. I worship Him because He is sovereign, endless and indestructible.

Let us make three observations about the role of "hope" in our lives;

1. We all depend on something or someone to hold us up inside. Whether you are a believer in Jesus Christ or not, you are counting on something or someone to support your life. That *something* or *someone* is your hope.

2. When the something or someone is "*coming through for us*", we are happy, very optimistic about the future and having a sense of satisfaction and peace. When thing are clicking and life is going well in the areas of your hope, you are at peace and you say, "Life is good".

3. When that something or someone "fails to come through for us", we become anxious, dissatisfied and very unhappy.

Hope can vanish in a heartbeat. Someone once said that hope is the oxygen of the soul. We can live for weeks without food, survive days without water, but without oxygen, we are only minutes from death.

Most of us don't like to think about what we are depending on. This is because when we do, we realize that our hopes are temporary and unreliable. The instability of everything around us makes us anxious. Wouldn't it be great to find something or someone that would always come through for us in any situation?

Where do you find that kind of person or that kind of hope? Because such a person must have certain attributes that will always come through for us no matter what. This person must be able to take care of our past, present and future. This person must have an indestructible and endless life.

Is there someone you can turn to when life isn't worth living, when your support system suddenly gets pulled out from under you? The only person that fits this profile is Jesus Christ, our great High Priest.

Whatever pain you are carrying and wherever you are, Christ's loving compassion is available for you. We have a compassionate High Priest with an endless life. You don't have to be afraid of your past, present or future because Jesus makes all things work together for your good (Romans 8:28).

The endless and indestructible life of our High Priest is the secret to a life of unending joy and peace. He is able to come through for you 100 percent in any and every situation forever.

This endless life of our great High Priest is backed with an oath. The old Aaronic priesthood perpetuated itself automatically from Father to Son. They became priests without any oath. But Jesus was made a High Priest forever with an oath.

What is an oath? It is a solemn promise to do something; or that something is true.

Those who formerly became priests received their office without a confirmation by oath before God. But Jesus was designated, addressed and saluted with an oath. The Lord God swore and will not regret it. He gave His word and won't take it back or change His mind.

Jesus Christ is a Priest forever (a permanent Priest) after the order of Melchizedek. In keeping with the oath's greater strength and force, Jesus has become the guarantee of a better, stronger, more excellent and advantageous covenant. Jesus made a surety of a better testament. Praise Jesus forever!

Brethren, His thoughts, intentions, desires and plans are always for your good and never for your harm. Jesus is actively and creatively orchestrating people, circumstances and events to express His affection and selective correction to provide for your highest good. Therefore, you can trust His intentions. Go to Him today, He has been waiting for you.

Jesus Christ Our Mediator

This book was birthed by a simple instruction one Sunday morning. I was about to give my offering to God then I heard in my spirit, *"offer that offering to your High Priest, Jesus Christ, Son of the living God"*. At that point, I knew that God was saying something to me. He asked me saying, *"Do you think you know the High Priest? Go, check who He is"*.

The following week, as I began to study Jesus, our High Priest, God whispered in my spirit, *"Go and introduce Me as High Priest to My children"*. From the very first page of this book, our focus has been on Jesus Christ. We saw Him in the Garden of Eden, in Noah, in Abraham, in Isaac, Jacob, the tabernacle of Moses and the Levitical priests. From Genesis to Revelation, Jesus has always been the focus.

I have tried to the best of my ability, to introduce you to your great High Priest, just as God instructed. Now I pray that through this revelation of Jesus Christ, you will experience Him fully as your High Priest in Jesus' Mighty Name.

Job 16:21

O that one might plead for a man with God, as a man [pleadeth] for his neighbour! (KJV)

Under the old covenant, the high priest was the legal representative of the people regarding spiritual matters. But there were many issues that the high priest could not arbitrate. Eli, when he was high priest in Israel, said the following;

1 Samuel 2:25a

If one man sin against another, the judge shall judge him: but if a man sin against the LORD, who shall intreat for him? (KJV)

Because of His Blood sacrifice, authority has been given unto Jesus as our legal mediator in heaven, representing us before the Father. He had in His hands, the only type of blood that could pacify the

Father for man's treason. His own Blood (Hebrews 9:12).

If Jesus had stopped with the substitutionary ministry, no one could ever be saved. He died as the Lamb, but arose as Lord and High Priest and entered His ministry as our Mediator.

1 Timothy 2:5

For there is only one God and one Mediator who can reconcile God and humanity-the man Christ Jesus.
(NLT)

Until we recognize Jesus Christ as our mediator, our relationship with the Father will amount to nothing; for no one can reach the Father except through Jesus.

John 14:6

Jesus saith unto him, I am the way, the truth, and the life: no man cometh unto the Father, but by me.
(KJV)

Having accepted Christ's full ministry, we can begin to make declarations with power and authority.

Jesus the Key to Answered Prayers

John 14:14

If ye shall ask any thing in my name, I will do [it].

(KJV)

Christ Jesus, our High Priest abolished all the Laws and rituals that held us bound in religion. Anytime we practice ritualistic worship, we are simply declaring that Jesus never came, never died, was never buried and never rose from the dead.

Could it be that in your life, Jesus never came? You may never admit it, but your actions, lifestyle and attitude to issues and circumstances betray you.

We must realize that salvation keeps speaking because of our High Priest. Christ's assignment as our High Priest is to keep our salvation ever new.

What is a ritual? It is a religious, pure or holy ceremony consisting of a series of actions performed according to a prescribed order. Keeping the laws and rituals never made them holy in the past, how could it achieve holiness now? Jesus came to absorb our old life, just as foam absorbs water. The Levitical priesthood, sacrifices, atonements and law code are no longer operative.

Jesus the Intercessor

Intercession means to meet with and to make petition.

It is Christ that died, yea rather, that is risen again. He is even at the right hand of God, making intercession for us. He is sitting at the place of highest honor next to the Father, pleading and praying for us non-stop. So who is he that condemns you? (Romans 8:34).

Hebrews 7:25

Wherefore he is able also to save them to the uttermost that come unto God by him, seeing he ever liveth to make intercession for them. (KJV)

The only reason Jesus can operate as our go-between in heaven is because He is both God and man. He alone can say, *"I know what man is like, and I know what God is like"*.

John 11:41

Then, to the others, "Go ahead, take away the stone." They removed the stone. Jesus raised his eyes to heaven and prayed, "Father, I'm grateful that you have listened to me. (MSG)

Jesus vouches for us and never forgets us. Do we think that it is our prayers that have kept us? No. Children of God, before we knew Him or how and what to pray for, Jesus had been praying for us.

Neither pray I for these alone, but for them also which shall believe on me through their word; (KJV)

Friends, He prayed for you before you ever prayed.

In chapter five, we spoke about the priestly garment. Aaron carried the names of the twelve (12) tribes of Israel on both his shoulders and chest. In the same vein, Christ carries us on His shoulders (His strength) and in His heart (His love) always; in the heaven, praying for us.

You can now understand why certain terrible things happen without affecting or causing you harm. You might have even forgotten to pray that day, but thank God we have someone constantly pleading our case before the Father.

Remember Peter who managed to fall short completely, all in one night (Luke 22:54-62). He made rash statements, acted impulsively, ran under pressure and denied Jesus. As much as we want to avoid Peter's sin, he is a good example of how God handles us.

Peter was so ashamed of himself, that he quit Jesus' ministry and went back to fishing (John 21). He didn't try to find Jesus or attempt to make things right. Yet Jesus, in His undying love, went looking for him and found him; just like He found you because you were the one that was lost. He did not only find you, He exchanged His life for yours so you are not merely changed, but exchanged. Hallelujah!

Jesus helped Peter unpack his guilt and set him free. This is the exact way He pursues us in love even after our mess-up, and leads us to restoration in Him. He prayed for Peter, that his faith would not fail.

Luke 22:31-32

And the Lord said, Simon, Simon, behold, Satan hath desired [to have] you, that he may sift [you] as wheat: But I have prayed for thee, that thy faith fail

You are Christ's attire. He wears you always in God's presence. Nothing happens by chance, there is always a propelling force behind every event. The prayers of Jesus are the propellants in the life of every true child of God. The word "coincidence" is not even in the Hebrew dictionary. Therefore, it is unhelpful to keep believing in the concept of coincidence. Nothing moves unless something moves it.

Over confidence in God must rise as we enter deeply into the reality of our glorious High Priest. The late Smith Wigglesworth, a powerful man of God, once saw the devil in his apartment and was not moved. Rather he said to the devil, *"I didn't even know it was you. Make sure you re-arrange my house and put everything in order as you met it, before you leave"*. Such boldness!

Oh I trust, believe in and totally rely on my High Priest. Anything can fail, not my High Priest. Jesus is in heaven right now, ministering God into your spirit man. As He ministers, you will experience His reality.

Don't ever imagine that you would enter the operating room and not come out alive and well. You have an intermediary in Christ. The Holy Spirit is also constantly praying for you, you are fully covered. Hallelujah!

That is why there are some types of prayers we should not pray. I was praying a particular prayer one day and the Lord told me to stop praying such prayers. He said, *"I have given you everything and done everything. I gave you my son"*.

Witness Lee in one of his books, said that when we come to the reality of Jesus Christ being our High Priest, we will realize that certain prayers are not necessary. We fight *from* victory, not *for* victory.

I had a particular vision where I saw myself before the Father and Jesus beside Him, praying for me. Suddenly, a thought dawned on me; *"What do I really do? He first loved me, came to the world because of me, died for me and rose for me. If I was the only one in the world, He would still die for me. Right now He is fighting both visible and invisible battles on my behalf, cheering me on this holy journey. He has prepared a place for me in eternity. What manner of love this is".*

I have never enjoyed my Christian walk the way I am right now. I am truly free; no doctrine, ritual or law code can cage me again. I am free indeed and I believe you are too. The Person who dwells in you as the Holy Spirit, is Jesus Christ Himself. He is also the One who approaches God daily as your High Priest.

His Mercy Endureth Forever

Psalm 103:8-13&17

The LORD [is] merciful and gracious, slow to anger, and plenteous in mercy. He will not always chide: neither will he keep [his anger] for ever. He hath not dealt with us after our sins; nor rewarded us according to our iniquities. For as the heaven is high above the earth, [so] great is his mercy toward them that fear him. As far as the east is from the west, [so] far hath he removed our transgressions from us. Like as a father pitieth [his] children, [so] the LORD pitieth them that fear him. But the mercy of the LORD [is] from everlasting to everlasting upon them that fear him, and his righteousness unto children's children;(KJV)

1 Chronicles 16:34

O give thanks unto the LORD; for [he is] good; for his mercy [endureth] for ever. (KJV)

Lamentations 3:22-23

[It is of] the LORD'S mercies that we are not consumed, because his compassions fail not. [They are] new every morning: great [is] thy faithfulness. (KJV)

One of our sisters sang a song about God's mercies; and suddenly I heard a question in my spirit, *"Why do you think my mercy endures forever?"*

The answer is that our High Priest is always there, keeping the mercy flowing. Imagine taking the High Priest out of the picture, it would be catastrophic.

Exodus 34:6

And the LORD passed by before him, and proclaimed, The LORD, The LORD God, merciful and gracious, longsuffering, and abundant in goodness and truth, (KJV)

All men are recipients of God's mercy. Do not think for a second that mercy began to operate as you repented and came back to the Father's house.

Matthew 5:45

That ye may be the children of your Father which is in heaven: for he maketh his sun to rise on the evil and on the good, and sendeth rain on the just and on the unjust. (KJV)

The Father makes His blessing available to both evil and good people alike. All of us are recipients of God's mercies including unbelievers.

I saw the Blood brethren, I saw the Blood; flowing from the throne of grace. I also saw the Lamb seated upon the throne and our Father looking at Him saying, *"You have paid for it all, with the Blood that makes mercy flow"*.

We can now appreciate scriptures like;

Hebrews 13:5c

I will never leave thee, nor forsake thee. (KJV)

Romans 8:28

And we know that all things work together for good to them that love God, to them who are the called according to [his] purpose. (KJV)

Matthew 11:28-30

Come unto me, all [ye] that labour and are heavy laden, and I will give you rest. Take my yoke upon you, and learn of me; for I am meek and lowly in heart: and ye shall find rest unto your souls. For my yoke [is] easy, and my burden is light. (KJV)

John 14:1

Let not your heart be troubled: ye believe in God, believe also in me. (KJV)

Our Advocate

Christ does more for us than being our Mediator. He is also our Advocate. Temptations and trials have caused many believers to fall out of fellowship with the Father. In the midst of their sorrow and grief, a true child of God suddenly remembers that Jesus is his advocate.

So he cries out, *"Father in Jesus' Name forgive and show me mercy"*. Our great advocate hears from heaven and says, *"Father, please lay that to my charge"*.

1 John 2:1-2

My little children, these things write I unto you, that ye sin not. And if any man sin, we have an advocate with the Father, Jesus Christ the righteous: And he is the propitiation for our sins: and not for ours only, but also for [the sins of] the whole world. (KJV)

Hallelujah to Jesus our advocate, our High Priest who makes appeals for us before the Father, thereby restoring our lost joy and right standing.

The devil's Distraction

2 Corinthians 12:6-10

For though I would desire to glory, I shall not be a fool; for I will say the truth: but [now] I forbear, lest any man should think of me above that which he seeth me [to be], or [that] he heareth of me. And lest I should be exalted above measure through the abundance of the revelations, there was given to me a thorn in the flesh, the messenger of Satan to buffet me, lest I should be exalted above measure. For this thing I besought the Lord thrice, that it might depart from me. And he said unto me, My grace is sufficient for thee: for my strength is made perfect in weakness. Most gladly therefore will I rather glory in my infirmities, that the power of Christ may rest upon me. Therefore I take pleasure in infirmities, in reproaches, in necessities, in persecutions, in distresses for Christ's sake: for when I am weak, then am I strong. (KJV)

Paul the Apostle was buffeted with a thorn, a splinter in his flesh to harass, torment and keep him from getting proud. Three times he asked and begged for it to depart, but the Lord told him to quit focusing on the handicap because His grace was sufficient.

In today's grammar, God said, *"Paul, you will be fine. Just continue with your assignment because these are all distractions"*. He continued thus; *"Paul, I am your great High Priest, I have done everything for you and opened a portal of strength for your weakness. I already took care of the pains you are feeling right now"*.

It is so hard for many christians to believe this because they do not understand eternity. God is eternal and cannot be compared to anything or anyone. *"Paul, I have finished all"*. Remember that Paul met Christ after His death and resurrection.

He was telling Paul to focus on Him as High Priest. *"Paul, I am your reality, not this thorn"*. Paul refused to be distracted. He carried on with the thorn for the rest of his life. He finished his assignment on earth, and finished well.

2 Timothy 4:7-8

I have fought a good fight, I have finished [my] course, I have kept the faith: Henceforth there is laid up for me a crown of righteousness, which the Lord, the righteous judge, shall give me at that day: and not to me only, but unto all them also that love his appearing. (KJV)

Just like Paul, everyone has a thorn in his or her flesh. We must learn to look away from this thorn and unto our High Priest. That thorn could be your financial status, an addiction, a weakness or what have you. Do not let it abort your glorious destiny.

God impacted Himself into Paul and gave him the grace to deny himself, carry his cross and follow Jesus till the end (Matthew 16:24).

Let us therefore hold fast to our confession, clinging in faith to all Jesus says. We have an anchor that keeps the soul, an anchor of hope, sure and steadfast. It cannot slip neither can it break under your weight. It is a hope that reaches farther and enters into the dwelling place of God. This anchor is an unbreakable spiritual life-line from God's inner sanctuary in heaven.

Hebrews 6:19

Which [hope] we have as an anchor of the soul, both sure and stedfast, and which entereth into that within the veil; (KJV)

The anchor of our hope is backed by the immutability of His counsel which He confirmed with an oath. Sure He would never change His mind, for it is impossible for God to lie or deceive us. We who fled to Him for refuge have that mighty indwelling strength and encouragement to hold fast and never let go of the hope appointed for us.

Everything we do must be in remembrance of Jesus Christ; this takes care of all ritualistic services and worship. We must remember all that He did for us, knowing that we owe Him our lives. Anything we do without Christ being our focus is simply religion and ritualistic. It is similar to confessing that Christ never died for us, because it denies His finished work.

Leader in All Things

The God-head never understood pain from the human angle. Nevertheless, when Jesus took on this physical body, He experienced our pain. He understands our weaknesses, feelings and circumstances which makes it impossible for Him to ignore our heartfelt prayers.

"He walked where I walk

He took my frailty

He understands

God with us, so close to us,

Emmanuel" – Don Moen

No man can ever know how you feel, because they cannot feel it. But Jesus knows and can feel it. No wonder it is by His stripes we are healed. He took a stripe for Covid 19 even before it appeared on earth, what a High Priest. That pain you feel is not your reality. Jesus your great High Priest is your reality.

Hallelujah!

PART FOUR

OUR PRIESTHOOD IN THE ORDER OF CHRIST

CHAPTER THIRTEEN

Priests Serving Under the High Priest

As our High Priest, Jesus has priests serving under Him. Who are these priests?

Revelation 1:6

And hath made us kings and priests unto God and his Father; to him [be] glory and dominion for ever and ever. Amen. (KJV)

As we serve as Priests under Jesus, we have to work the way He works.

In the Old Testament, regular priests were not allowed into the holy of holies, only the High Priest. In this new covenant however, we serve with Jesus right inside the holy of holies.

Ephesians 2:6

And He raised us up together with Him and made us sit down together [giving us joint seating with Him] in the heavenly sphere [by virtue of our being] in Christ Jesus (the Messiah, the Anointed One). (AMP)

The Old covenant is miles apart from this new and better one. Indeed we are blessed to be partakers of our Father's new covenant. We are a fulfillment of the scripture which says that old things are passed away and all things are new (2 Corinthians 5:17).

Diverse Gifts

If Christ is right now at the right hand of the Father, carrying out His manifold ministry, our works here on earth should be manifold as well because He works through us. His work in us is expressed through diverse gifts.

1 Corinthians 12:4

Now there are distinctive varieties and distributions of endowments (gifts, extraordinary powers distinguishing certain Christians, due to the power of divine grace operating in their souls by the Holy Spirit) and they vary, but the [Holy] Spirit remains the same. (AMP)

1 Corinthians 12:8-11

for to one is given the word of wisdom through the Spirit, to another the word of knowledge through the same Spirit, to another faith by the same Spirit, to another gifts of healings by the same Spirit, to another the working of miracles, to another prophecy, to another discerning of spirits, to another different kinds of tongues, to another the interpretation of tongues. But one and the same Spirit works all these things, distributing to each one individually as He wills. (NKJV)

Therefore, we serve as priests as we utilize these diverse gifts for the advancement of God's kingdom here on earth, thereby engaging actively in Christ's manifold work.

The grace of our Lord Jesus Christ is multi-dimensional in nature. That is why we can do all things through Christ (Philippians 4:13). The things we can do are not the same, but we can do all. Hence Jesus said to the disciples that is was better for Him to leave.

John 16:7

Nevertheless I tell you the truth. It is to your advantage that I go away; for if I do not go away, the Helper will not come to you; but if I depart, I will send Him to you. (NKJV)

Now Jesus is here with us in the person of the Holy Spirit.

The State of Believers Today

Very sadly, believers are hardly aware of our High Priest. As priests, we have unconsciously exalted ourselves above and beyond our High Priest, and crowded Him out. We have even accepted the praise and glorification of men, which Jesus utterly rejected.

John 6:15

Jesus saw that in their enthusiasm, they were about to grab him and make him king, so he slipped off and went back up the mountain to be by himself. (MSG)

If Jesus rejected the glorification of men, why do we crave for it? We are probably unaware. That is why this book has been written, to help us operate like Christ, not otherwise.

Mark 10:17-18

As he went out into the street, a man came running up, greeted him with great reverence, and asked,

"Good Teacher, what must I do to get eternal life?"
Jesus said, "Why are you calling me good? No one is
good, only God. (MSG)

Jesus quickly stopped anyone from calling Him good, meanwhile as Priests serving under Him, many of us are approval and praise addicts. Is it a wonder that we are void of power and exploits? We are hardly following the lead of our High Priest. Our mindset must be renewed and aligned to that of Jesus, for us to experience God's power.

What the praise of men does is to blind us from the mannerisms of Christ's manifold work. Many believers are now caught in the web of acting other than Christ. Anytime we assume and accept a position that Jesus never did, we contradict our Christian faith.

Grace versus Works

Ephesians 2:8-9

For it is by free grace (God's unmerited favor) that you are saved (delivered from judgment and made partakers of Christ's salvation) through [your] faith. And this [salvation] is not of yourselves [of your own doing, it came not through your own striving], but it is the gift of God; Not because of works [not the fulfillment of the Law's demands], lest any man should boast. [It is not the result of what anyone can possibly do, so no one can pride himself in it or take glory to himself.] (AMP)

Another sad state of many believers today is boastfulness. We should never be caught in the trap of boasting in the works of our hands. Every gift that we operate is released to us by God's free grace. We must be humbled by God's gift upon our lives, not otherwise.

Philippians 2:5-7

Think of yourselves the way Christ Jesus thought of himself. He had equal status with God but didn't think so much of himself that he had to cling to the advantages of that status no matter what. Not at all. When the time came, he set aside the privileges of deity and took on the status of a slave, became human! (MSG)

As priests we must imitate Christ.

Ephesians 5:1

THEREFORE BE imitators of God [copy Him and follow His example], as well-beloved children [imitate their father]. (AMP)

We embrace the grace to be imitators of our High Priest in Jesus' Mighty Name. Amen.

CHAPTER FOURTEEN
Our Call to Priesthood

One of the duties of a priest, as pointed out in chapter three, is to mediate between man and God. In Genesis, God enjoyed fellowship directly with man, without the need for a mediator.

Genesis 3:8

And they heard the sound of the Lord God walking in the garden in the cool of the day ... (AMP)

However, after the fall man was disconnected from fellowship with God, giving rise to the need for reconciliation. This began the advent of priesthood.

Our service and offerings to God as priests ought to be characterized by excellence, just like Abel.

Hebrews 11:4

[Prompted, actuated] by faith Abel brought God a better and more acceptable sacrifice than Cain, because of which it was testified of him that he was righteous [that he was upright and in right standing with God], and God bore witness by accepting and acknowledging his gifts. And though he died, yet [through the incident] he is still speaking. (AMP)

There is so much to learn from the contrast between the offerings of Cain and Abel. This is in order to avoid the danger of making the same mistake that Cain made in offering an unacceptable sacrifice to God.

Priestly Sacrifices

1 Peter 2:5

And you are living stones that God is building into his spiritual temple. What's more, you are his holy

priests. Through the mediation of Jesus Christ, you offer spiritual sacrifices that please God .(NLT)
Another priestly duty involves performing sacred rituals of religion. In the Old Covenant, this involved animal sacrifices. God never has need to fill His belly with our sacrifices. Our sacrifices only point to our recognition of God as Lord in our lives. The New Covenant suggests that we are to present ourselves as sacrifices unto God in the order of Jesus.

Romans 12:1

I APPEAL to you therefore, brethren, and beg of you in view of [all] the mercies of God, to make a decisive dedication of your bodies [presenting all your members and faculties] as a living sacrifice, holy (devoted, consecrated) and well pleasing to God, which is your reasonable (rational, intelligent) service and spiritual worship. (AMP)

To fully grasp this revelation, we must first understand fully, the constituents of the sacrifice of Jesus.

Jesus the Ultimate Sacrifice

The difference between Jesus and other high priests of old is that He became the sacrifice. While the other high priests offered up burnt offerings to God, Jesus laid Himself on the altar, and became the burnt offering.

It is commonly heard amongst us believers that the roman soldiers killed Jesus, and not we ourselves. How so? The ultimate reason that Jesus came to earth was to die for our sake. Therefore if not for us, Jesus wouldn't have needed to die. We did kill Jesus.

Furthermore, Jesus laid himself on the altar of sacrifice to be slain. For every sacrifice, there had to be a priest to slaughter the animal. As ordained priest and kings, we carried out the slaughter, not the unbelievers. Any believer that refuses to accept this truth will never enjoy Christ fully.

Now that Jesus has been offered up to God as the ultimate sacrifice, there is no need for any other sacrifice because now we live as sacrifices ourselves.

We are now priests expected to function in the order of Jesus Christ. The order of Jesus was to be the ultimate sacrifice. He came to set the ultimate example of sacrificial life. Jesus shed His blood as the last blood sacrifice, to open up the holy of holies forever. There is no longer any need for blood sacrifices. Placing higher priority over other people's needs as against ours, is a call to live sacrificially.

I cannot present myself as a living sacrifice unto God, if I am not yet one with the person that became the ultimate sacrifice. I cannot claim to be one with the High Priest, and not also be a sacrifice. Being a sacrifice means being sold out to sacrificial living as in the Beatitudes in Matthew 5:1-12.

Now that I am one with Him, it means that the day that Jesus Christ was sacrificed, I was also sacrificed.

Galatians 2:20

I have been crucified with Christ [in Him I have shared His crucifixion]; it is no longer I who live, but Christ (the Messiah) lives in me ... (AMP)

This is the gospel! We are ordained to be living sacrifices unto God. We might as well dive into this revelation and live out its implications in our everyday lives.

Christ is our High Priest in the order of Melchizedek, and we are now priests in the order of Christ.

The Mind of Jesus

The idea of priesthood is so alluring that unfortunately, many servants of God have become trapped in greed. They prefer to be priests in the order of Melchizedek, so as to collect the tithes. What differentiates Jesus from the high priests of old is that He never focused on collecting from the people. Rather He gave even to the point of giving His own life.

The mind of Jesus was that of giving and not receiving, just like our heavenly Father. For God so loved the world that He gave (John 3:16). Even after performing diverse miracles, He never demanded an offering. He always directed the beneficiaries to the priest (Luke 5:14). He never even sought recognition for Himself, but for the Father. This should be our mindset as priests in His order.

Any priest that is not out to give, is not in the order of Christ. The Lord said this to me some time ago; *"Child you are too full. I cannot fill you up until you empty yourself".* This was in terms of scriptural revelation. Many servants of God are so full, that they have begun to stink like stagnant water.

The Old Testament spirit is still very much alive amongst countless believers today. That spirit is one that collects and collects without ever giving. The Old Testament priests knew nothing more than to receive people's offerings. However, the new and better covenant is one of giving, in God's order (John 3:16).

Sadly, many pastors have tagged some members of their congregation as unworthy, according to the size of their *"meagre donations"*. While God is in search of true shepherds that would feed His children, countless servants of God have chased many away because their pocket sizes were not large enough. Very sad indeed.

Based on the above, it is obvious that several servants of God are lost. The Old covenant has been passed down several generations and is tough to break out of. This was the case with the Pharisees and Sadducees in Jesus' days on earth.

Matthew 23:13

"I've had it with you! You're hopeless, you religion scholars, you Pharisees! Frauds! Your lives are roadblocks to God's kingdom. You refuse to enter, and won't let anyone else in either. (MSG)

May we never be roadblocks in God's kingdom in Jesus' Name.

CHAPTER FIFTEEN

You Are a Priest in the Order Of Christ

Now that we know Jesus Christ as our High Priest, and we are priests serving under Him, we must now take responsibility and rise to our positions in Him.

Any scriptural revelation that does not leave you with a responsibility, is mere information; like reading a newspaper. A true revelation leaves the benefactor with action steps. These steps are meant to be carried out fully, before their results begin to manifest. The benefits of a true revelation will never be enjoyed unless those necessary steps are taken.

If for example, you received a revelation from God about singing in the choir, and your voice needs some work, the responsible thing is to begin to train your voice.

In the same vein, the Lord has revealed to us from scriptures that we are priests in the order of Jesus. The responsible thing to do is dive in immediately and prayerfully.

The list of necessary attributes are definitely inexhaustible, but we would like to point out a few of them below.

New Covenant Necessities

1. **A life of Sacrifice**

Hebrews 13:15

Through Him, therefore, let us constantly and at all times offer up to God a sacrifice of praise, which is the fruit of lips that thankfully acknowledge and confess and glorify His name. (AMP)

2. Self-denial

Luke 9:23

Then He said to them all, "If anyone desires to come after Me, let him deny himself, and take up his cross daily, and follow Me. (NKJV)

Just like Jesus denied Himself, the privileges of deity, we must also deny ourselves of fleshly desires and truly follow Him.

3. Servant-hood

Matthew 20:25-28

So Jesus got them together to settle things down. He said, "You've observed how godless rulers throw their weight around, how quickly a little power goes to their heads. It's not going to be that way with you. Whoever wants to be great must become a servant. Whoever wants to be first among you must be your slave. That is what the Son of Man has done: He came to serve, not be served--and then to give away his life in exchange for the many who are held hostage." (MSG)

The life of priesthood after the order of Christ is not one of lording authority over others, but one of being a servant.

4. Spiritual Maturity

Hebrews 5:12

For even though by this time you ought to be teaching others, you actually need someone to teach you over again the very first principles of God's Word. You have come to need milk, not solid food.

(AMP)

The Old covenant consisted of endless rituals and rule keeping. Sadly, many denominational doctrines are neck deep in such practices. The doctrine of handkerchiefs for example is keeping many believers stuck in babyhood.

Acts 19:11-12

Now God worked unusual miracles by the hands of Paul, so that even handkerchiefs or aprons were brought from his body to the sick, and the diseases left them and the evil spirits went out of them.
(NKJV)

Handkerchiefs were taken from Paul's body to heal the sick. When will we grow up to the level of dishing out handkerchiefs to heal others? The choice to grow up is ours.

Every child of God is ordained a priest to serve under our great High Priest. When He calls we answer. Whatever instruction he gives, we carry out with all our hearts and strength. The only person we owe on earth is Jesus. Therefore we must not allow anything or anyone to separate us from the one who paid such a high price for our souls.

Romans 8:35-37

Who shall separate us from the love of Christ? [shall] tribulation, or distress, or persecution, or famine, or nakedness, or peril, or sword? As it is written, For thy sake we are killed all the day long; we are accounted as sheep for the slaughter. Nay, in all these things we are more than conquerors through him that loved us. (KJV)

PRAYER POINT

Father in the Name of Jesus, please help us to operate fully as priests in the order of Christ Jesus Your son, our savior and great High Priest. In Jesus' most precious Name. Amen.

CONCLUSION

Believe in Your High Priest

John 4:1-30 tells the story of Christ's encounter with a Samaritan woman at Jacob's well. In their conversation, Jesus used the word "worship" or "worshipper" seven times. He made it clear that worship is not about a place, but it flows from the Spirit and Truth knowing God Himself.

In just a few moments, Jesus forever altered the woman's view of God. She began to see God in a deeper, wider and truer way; and also thought of herself differently. This encounter with Jesus transformed her into a persuasive witness.

John 4:28-30

The woman then left her waterpot, and went her way into the city, and saith to the men, Come, see a man, which told me all things that ever I did: is not this the Christ? Then they went out of the city, and came unto him. (KJV)

We started this journey into the Priesthood of Jesus, by pointing out the significance of the way we see Him. Jesus opened the eyes of the Samaritan woman to realize that there was so much more to knowing God, than her local tradition had taught her. He gave her an answer to the deep longing of her soul.

She caught a glimpse of Jesus as the exact representation of God and the embodiment of the fullness of God. Jesus was good to her and genuinely concerned for her welfare. He was just, not letting the judgment of man affect His mercy towards her. He dealt honestly and fairly with her from an eternal perspective.

He was loving and patient in answering her questions, seeking her salvation above all else. He was so faithful that He carried out His will for an entire community through the witness of one saved soul.

He clothed Himself in humanity in order to demonstrate exactly who He is. His desire is for us to see Him as our High Priest, and come up higher to the level of engaging actively as priests in His order.

The chapters were prayerfully written to help us understand the implication of Jesus Christ being our High Priest. Now that we are aware of what we have in Jesus, we must not let it slip through our fingers. We must cling to Him and never stop trusting Him. He understands, sympathizes and shares in the feeling of our weakness, infirmity and liability to the assault of temptation; experiencing it all but without sinning.

Let us fearlessly, confidently and boldly draw near to the throne of God's grace and unmerited favor to us sinners; walking right up to Him to receive all that He is so ready to give. Let us take the mercy that is freely available and accept His help.

May the Lord Bless you and keep you.
The Lord make His face shine upon you and be gracious to you.
The Lord lift up His countenance upon you and give you peace. Amen

We serve a God who wants to be believed. Only believe. All things are possible to them that believe. Jesus Christ the great High Priest is our reality!

ABOUT THE AUTHOR

Watchmaidens Ministry is a Christian interdenominational Para – Church Mission organization, based in Lagos, Nigeria. Founded in September, 2011, Watchmaidens has a clear and strong intercessory mandate anchored on the Word of God, and the vision to pray for the body of Christ, "The Church", the Nations of the world, lost souls and the lost in the Church.

To the glory of God, we have thus far been empowered by the grace of God to stand in this intercessory assignment. Now the Lord has birthed yet another book as a baby born out of a deep passion to see Christians re-acquainted with Christ as our High Priest, thereby being restored to the original image of God. A Church without spot or wrinkle.

www.ingramcontent.com/pod-product-compliance
Lightning Source LLC
Chambersburg PA
CBHW050508160726
48003CB00001B/221